I0818169

MARK TWAIN FOR HORSE LOVERS

The Genuine Mexican Plug.

MARK TWAIN FOR HORSE LOVERS

True and Imaginary Adventures
WITH HORSES AND THEIR KIN

Edited by

R. KENT RASMUSSEN

ESSEX, CONNECTICUT

An imprint of The Globe Pequot Publishing Group, Inc.
64 South Main St.
Essex, CT 06426
www.GlobePequot.com

British Library Cataloguing in Publication Information Available

Library of Congress Cataloging-in-Publication Data Available

ISBN 9781493091720 (cloth : alk. paper) | ISBN 9781493091737 (epub)

For Shelley Fisher Fishkin, a treasured friend
whose countless contributions to Mark Twain studies
include the most comprehensive work ever published
on Mark Twain and animals.

CONTENTS

INTRODUCTION

Anyone imagining Mark Twain with an animal is likely to conjure an image of him fondly stroking a cat and, if not a cat, perhaps a dog. Mark Twain is well known to have been passionate about cats, and his affection for dogs is also no secret. Did he also love horses? Perhaps not so much—but wait. The fact is that Mark Twain had an affectionate regard for almost *all* animals, and he played an active role in looking out for their welfare. That is not altogether surprising for a writer whose rise to fame began with a story about a frog—which, incidentally, was owned by a gambler who also owned an unusual horse that readers meet later in these pages. What may be surprising is how *much* he wrote about horses—at least as much as he wrote about cats and dogs combined. Also surprising is what he had to say about them. In fact, he even wrote a book about a horse. He did the same thing for a dog but never for a cat! Both the dog and horse books he wrote for the express purpose of promoting animal welfare.

The numbers of people who own horses are only a small fraction of those who own dogs and cats, but that means little when it comes to how many people love horses—even people who have never been near a real horse. The reasons people love horses are also more diverse than the reasons people love such pets as cats and dogs. Horses have played an outsize role in Western civilization and consequently loom large in our collective consciousness. They have long performed such prosaic tasks as hauling goods and pulling plows and milk wagons, as well as more glamorous and romantic tasks, such as pulling dashing chariots and frontier stagecoaches; carrying medieval knights and modern cavalry into battle; providing mounts for cowboys, American Indians, and bandits of the Old West; and making possible thoroughbred racing. Not coincidentally, Mark Twain has something interesting and fun to say

A HORSE'S TALE

MARK TWAIN

about most of those pursuits. Incidentally, readers will find what he says about a milk-wagon horse to be as entertaining as what he says about the mighty steeds of sixth-century English knights.

It may be a stretch to call Mark Twain himself a lover of horses, but as shown in the following pages, there can be no doubt that he admired and respected the animals, and he may even be said to have stood in awe of them. True horse lovers don't need to be told that horses are awesome creatures. Imposingly tall, powerful, handsome, and intelligent, they are also fast—so fast, in fact, that for thousands of years they provided the speediest transportation available to human beings. They have many qualities that are superior to those of humans—something that Mark Twain clearly understood. Throughout the pages that follow are acknowledgments of that truth testifying to his high regard for the animals.

Among the many reasons for reading Mark Twain is the pure joy provided by his humor. Readers will find plenty of horse laughs in these pages, but those who really understand and appreciate horses will also find something more. Mark Twain had exceptional powers of observation. He notices things that others may overlook and calls attention to unexpected details in compelling and typically humorous ways. For example, how many writers would think to comment on a horse that preserves its self-possession in the presence of a barley sack? And who else can make such a sentence sound compelling? Experienced equestrians will appreciate the authenticity of his descriptions of what it feels like to mount a horse—especially for riders uncomfortable with the challenges riding horses pose. Let's admit it: Riding a big, powerful horse can be daunting, and a steed's size is not the only thing that can make horseback riding intimidating. As Mark Twain says in one of the last selections in this volume, "The horse has too many caprices, and he is too much given to initiative. He invents too many new ideas." In other words, riding a horse can be like riding in a car driven by an artificial intelligence program that doesn't always want to go where you want to go. Mark Twain rode a lot of horses with a similar attitude.

Born in 1835 as Samuel Langhorne Clemens and raised on the fringe of America's western frontier during the mid-nineteenth century, Mark Twain lived most of his life in close proximity to horses, mules, and donkeys.* It should be kept in mind, however, that the same thing may also be said about most Americans of his time—even those living in such crowded urban centers as New York. Because humans depended on them in so many different ways, horses were everywhere. Mark Twain encountered and observed horses in most of their diverse roles. He lived through the crest of the Industrial Revolution that would eventually diminish the roles of horses; however, until the perfection of internal combustion engines toward the tail end of the nineteenth century, horses were the main engines of land-based transportation and drayage and did the heaviest labor on the farms that fed the nation and drove its economy. The same was true for most of the many places throughout the world that Mark Twain visited.

While Mark Twain was near horses throughout his entire life, the period during which he rode them the most was the 1860s, when he traveled, prospected, and worked in the Far West and in the kingdom of Hawaii and traveled in Europe and the Middle East. During those years, he frequently rode equine animals, and when not straddling a saddle or riding in a train, he typically traveled in horse-drawn coaches, carriages, or carts. He lived long enough to see the machinery and vehicles of the Industrial Revolution begin to push horses aside, but the animals remained important to him right up until his death in 1910.

ORGANIZATION OF THIS BOOK

The texts in this volume are arranged under nine loosely thematic subject headings, within which individual selections are arranged in a more or less chronological order that may help readers observe the evolution of Mark Twain's views about the subjects. The overall arrangement is not meant to be rigid, as many selections could easily fall under more than one heading. The very first selection, for example, "Saddle Up!" describes Mark Twain's quasi-military experience at the start of the Civil War and would fit nicely in part VIII, "War Horses." It is instead in part I, "Uneasy Rider," because it is about his earliest formal training in horsemanship, and it introduces the basis for his lifelong diffidence about mastering that skill. Other selections in part I carry that theme

* To avoid having to repeat this phrase, the word *horse* is often used to encompass true horses; their closely related equine kin, donkeys; and their hybrid cousins, mules.

through later experiences in his history of horseback riding and include his celebrated memoir about the "Genuine Mexican Plug."

Part II, "Happy Trails," changes directions slightly with selections about Mark Twain's more pleasant equine encounters and observations of other riders. Part III then shifts to tales of "Horse Traders," who, not surprisingly, tend to be rather shifty. Part IV, "Sorry Steeds," returns to the theme of Mark Twain's diffidence about riding by focusing on a number of sad but often hilarious animals he struggled to ride. Part V, "Eccentric Equines," then takes a more positive turn with stories about exceptional horses truly worthy of admiration—or at least of wonderment. Part VI, "Daredevil Riders," turns the focus from the animals to the people who rode them. Its selections include a letter to the famous showman Buffalo Bill, in which Mark Twain relates a brief but poignant recollection of the moment he rode his Genuine Mexican Plug many years earlier—a moment in when he justly deserved to be called a daredevil himself! Part VII, "Unhappy Horsey Happenstances," offers examples of accidents and other mishaps Mark Twain and other riders had with their mounts. The true (or allegedly true) and fictional stories in Part VIII, "War Horses," are not so much about actual warfare—which Mark Twain himself never really experienced—as they are about people and animals trained for war. They also include an anecdote about a moment when Mark Twain found himself involved in preparing for potential combat, as well as the previously quoted anecdote about the "caprices" of horses. Finally, Part IX, "Closer to Home and Family," rounds up a variety of reminiscences—mostly from Mark Twain's later years—that involve his family members (several are written by his daughter Clara). Its first selection, "Milk Run," involves no other family members but is set close to his home, though *which* home is difficult to say. The section's final piece, about a Bermuda donkey named Maude, contains some of Mark Twain's final words about equines. Appropriately, those words are entirely favorable.

GOALS OF THIS BOOK

This book has several objectives. First, it reveals a side of Mark Twain that is little known despite the fact that it encompasses nearly his entire life. Indeed, this book might even be read as a form of his life history, seen through the perspective of his fraught relationship with horses.

This book also serves as a window into a past time, when horses played vital roles in human civilization. The anecdotes in this volume illuminate the uses of horses from the mid-nineteenth into the very early twentieth centuries, but it should be remembered that horses were even more important during earlier centuries, before the nineteenth-century development of steam engines made possible steam-powered trains, ships, and machinery. A final goal of this volume is simply to entertain. The texts collected here are nothing if not a great deal of fun, and they can be enjoyed without having to give a single thought to any loftier reasons for reading them.

Cathy, astride Soldier Boy, and Buffalo Bill in A Horse's Tale.

A NOTE ON TEXTS

Aside from several noted exceptions, all the texts in this book were written by Mark Twain and are rendered here as they were originally published, complete with his occasionally irregular spellings and often eccentric punctuation. Gaps in the texts are marked with ellipses. Mark Twain wrote about horses in a wide variety of his publications, all of which are clearly identified here. About half the texts are taken from his five travel books, most notably *The Innocents Abroad* (1869) and *Roughing It* (1872), which cover the years when he did most of his horseback riding. A half-dozen items come from contemporary newspapers for which he wrote travel letters. Several of these letters are used here because they present fuller accounts than their corresponding chapters in the travel books.

Horses figure less prominently in Mark Twain's fiction than one might expect, so only a few texts from his novels are extracted here. The fact is that his most interesting writings about the animals can be found in what he says about his own firsthand experiences. Readers should, however, be aware that many passages he presents as personal memoirs are either highly embellished or outright fiction. His most reliable nonfiction accounts are doubtless the personal letters he wrote, five of which appear here. Finally, several texts are taken from books by other writers, including Mark Twain's daughter Clara. These passages are included because they offer poignant anecdotes about moments in Mark Twain's life.

"I never mount a horse without experiencing a sort of dread that I may be setting out on that last mysterious journey which all of us must take sooner or later."

PART I

UNEASY RIDER

First, let it be confessed that although Mark Twain was frequently in the company of horses throughout his life, he was rarely completely comfortable riding them. He grew up in Hannibal, Missouri, a riverfront village then on the fringe of the western frontier, and spent most of his summers at his uncle's inland farm, where he must have encountered horses, donkeys, and mules. He probably rode some of those animals and certainly traveled in wagons and carts pulled by them, but he seems not to have recorded whatever equine encounters he had in his youth.

During the years leading up to the Civil War, he was busy piloting steamboats on the Mississippi River and would have had few occasions to ride horses. After the war started, however, everything changed. Over the next seven years, he found himself often riding horses, mules, and donkeys—typically with something less than enthusiasm. He was not exaggerating when he described himself as a diffident rider. This section offers a selection of his firsthand accounts of his early riding experiences.

LEARNING PAINS

"Stevens's horse would carry him, when he was not noticing, under the huge excrescences which form on the trunks of oak-trees, and wipe him out of the saddle."

1

SADDLE UP!

In 1885, Mark Twain published a highly embellished memoir for a magazine series of wartime memoirs by Civil War leaders, though he himself was not a Civil War leader. In fact, the exact nature of his Civil War experience is unclear. His article describes how the start of the war ended his piloting career, leaving him to join a band of inexperienced comrades responding to a call to form a militia unit as Union forces were occupying Missouri. Whether the "Marion Rangers" his article describes really existed or whether he can be said to have served the Confederacy (which Missouri never joined) are open questions. What matters here is that the article may describe Mark Twain's first serious attempt to master horsemanship.

We occupied an old maple-sugar camp, whose half-rotted troughs were still propped against the trees. A long corn-crib served for sleeping-quarters for the battalion. On our left, half a mile away, were Mason's farm and house; and he was a friend to the cause. Shortly after noon the farmers began to arrive from several directions, with mules and horses for our use, and these they lent us for as long as the war might last, which they judged would be about three months. The animals were of all sizes, all colors, and all breeds. They were mainly young and frisky, and nobody in the command could stay on them long at a time; for we were town boys, and ignorant of horsemanship. The creature that fell to my share was a very small mule, and yet so quick and active that it could throw me without difficulty; and it did this whenever I got on it. Then it would bray—stretching its neck out, laying its ears back, and spreading its jaws till you could see down to its works. It was a disagreeable animal in every way. If I took it by the bridle and tried to lead it off the grounds, it would sit down and brace back, and no one could budge it. However, I was not entirely destitute of military resources, and I did presently manage to spoil this game; for I had seen many a steamboat aground in my time, and knew a trick or two which even a grounded mule would be obliged to respect. There was a well by the corn-crib; so I substituted thirty fathom of rope for the bridle, and fetched him home with the windlass.

I will anticipate here sufficiently to say that we did learn to ride, after some days' practice, but never well. We could not learn to like our animals; they were not choice ones, and most of them had annoying

Town boys learning horsemanship.

peculiarities of one kind or another. Stevens's horse would carry him, when he was not noticing, under the huge excrescences which form on the trunks of oak-trees, and wipe him out of the saddle; in this way Stevens got several bad hurts. Sergeant Bowers's horse was very large and tall, with slim, long legs, and looked like a railroad bridge. His size enabled him to reach all about, and as far as he wanted to, with his head; so he was always biting Bowers's legs. On the march, in the sun, Bowers slept a good deal; and as soon as the horse recognized that he was asleep he would reach around and bite him on the leg. His legs were black and blue with bites. This was the only thing that could ever make him swear, but this always did; whenever his horse bit him he always swore, and of course Stevens, who laughed at everything, laughed at this, and would

Though small, Mark Twain's mule could throw him without difficulty.

even get into such convulsions over it as to lose his balance and fall off his horse; and then Bowers, already irritated by the pain of the horse-bite, would resent the laughter with hard language, and there would be a quarrel; so that horse made no end of trouble and bad blood in the command.

However, I will get back to where I was—our first afternoon in the sugar-camp. The sugar-troughs came very handy as horse-troughs, and we had plenty of corn to fill them with. I ordered Sergeant Bowers to feed my mule; but he said that if I reckoned he went to war to be a dry-nurse to a mule it wouldn't take me very long to find out my mistake. I believed that this was insubordination, but I was full of uncertainties about everything military, and so I let the thing pass, and went and ordered Smith, the blacksmith's apprentice, to feed the mule; but he merely gave me a large, cold, sarcastic grin, such as an ostensibly seven-year-old horse gives you when you lift his lip and find he is fourteen, and turned his back on me. I then went to the captain, and asked if it were not right and proper and military for me to have an orderly. He said it was, but as there was only one orderly in the corps, it was but right that he himself should have Bowers on his staff. Bowers said he wouldn't serve on anybody's staff; and if anybody thought he could make him, let him try it. So, of course, the thing had to be dropped; there was no other way.

We had some horsemanship drill every forenoon; then, afternoons, we rode off here and there in squads a few miles, and visited the farmers' girls, and had a youthful good time, and got an honest good dinner or supper, and then home again to camp, happy and content.

—"The Private History of a Campaign That Failed" (1885)

2

THE GENUINE MEXICAN PLUG

Mark Twain's military adventure lasted only a few weeks. His next move was to go west with his brother Orion, recently appointed secretary of the new Nevada Territory. Leaving Missouri freed him from having to take sides in the Civil War, with the added possibility of getting rich by prospecting for silver. He and Orion had an exciting time crossing the plains in a horse-drawn stagecoach. On his arrival in Carson City, one of the first things he wanted to do was to buy a horse. That made sense; he had to have some means to get around. What happened next sounds incredible, but most of it is apparently true. Not surprisingly, this is Mark Twain's best-known horse story.

I resolved to have a horse to ride. I had never seen such wild, free, magnificent horsemanship outside of a circus as these picturesquely clad Mexicans, Californians and Mexicanized Americans displayed in Carson streets every day. How they rode! Leaning just gently forward out of the perpendicular, easy and nonchalant, with broad slouch-hat brim blown square up in front, and long riata swinging above the head, they swept through the town like the wind! The next minute they were only a sailing puff of dust on the far desert. If they trotted, they sat up gallantly and gracefully, and seemed part of the horse; did not go jiggering up and down after the silly Miss-Nancy fashion of the riding-schools. I had quickly learned to tell a horse from a cow, and was full of anxiety to learn more. I was resolved to buy a horse.

While the thought was rankling in my mind, the auctioneer came skurrying through the plaza on a black beast that had as many humps and corners on him as a dromedary, and was necessarily uncomely; but he was "going, going, at twenty-two!—horse, saddle and bridle at twenty-two dollars, gentlemen!" and I could hardly resist.

A man whom I did not know (he turned out to be the auctioneer's brother) noticed the wistful look in my eye, and observed that that was a very remarkable horse to be going at such a price; and added that the saddle alone was worth the money. It was a Spanish saddle, with ponderous tapidaros [stirrup covers], and furnished with the ungainly sole-leather covering with the unspellable name. I said I had half a notion to bid. Then this keen-eyed person appeared to me to be "taking my measure"; but I dismissed the suspicion when he spoke, for his manner was full of guileless candor and truthfulness. Said he:

"I know that horse—know him well. You are a stranger, I take it, and so you might think he was an American horse, maybe, but I assure you he is not. He is nothing of the kind; but—excuse my speaking in a low voice, other people being near—he is, without the shadow of a doubt, a Genuine Mexican Plug!"

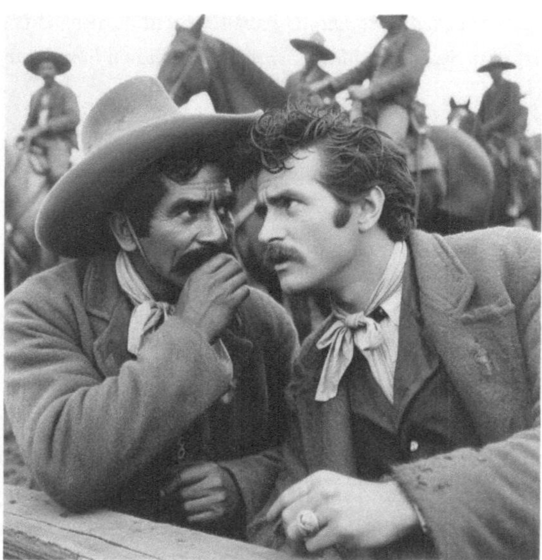

The auctioneer's brother speaking with guileless candor and truthfulness.

I did not know what a Genuine Mexican Plug was, but there was something about this man's way of saying it, that made me swear inwardly that I would own a Genuine Mexican Plug, or die.

"Has he any other—er—advantages?" I inquired, suppressing what eagerness I could.

He hooked his forefinger in the pocket of my army-shirt, led me to one side, and breathed in my ear impressively these words:

"He can out-buck anything in America!"

"Going, going, going—at twent-ty-four dollars and a half, gen—"

"Twenty-seven!" I shouted, in a frenzy.

"And sold!" said the auctioneer, and passed over the Genuine Mexican Plug to me.

I could scarcely contain my exultation. I paid the money, and put the animal in a neighboring livery-stable to dine and rest himself.

In the afternoon I brought the creature into the plaza, and certain citizens held him by the head, and others by the tail, while I mounted him. As soon as they let go, he placed all his feet in a bunch together, lowered his back, and then suddenly arched it upward, and shot me straight into the air a matter of three or four feet! I came as straight down again, lit in the saddle, went instantly up again, came down almost on the high pommel, shot up again, and came down on the horse's neck—all in the space of three or four seconds. Then he rose and stood almost straight up on his hind feet, and I, clasping his lean neck desperately, slid back into the saddle, and held on. He came down, and immediately hoisted his heels into the air, delivering a vicious kick at the sky, and stood on his forefeet. And then down he came once more, and began the original exercise of shooting me straight up again. The third time I went up I heard a stranger say:

"Oh, don't he buck, though!"

While I was up, somebody struck the horse a sounding thwack with a leathern strap, and when I arrived again the Genuine Mexican Plug was not there. A Californian youth chased him up and caught him, and asked if he might have a ride. I granted him that luxury. He mounted the Genuine, got lifted into the air once, but sent his spurs home as he descended, and the horse darted away like a telegram. He soared over three fences like a bird, and disappeared down the road toward the Washoe Valley.

The moment Mark Twain mounts the Mexican plug, he is shot straight up into the air.

I sat down on a stone, with a sigh, and by a natural impulse one of my hands sought my forehead, and the other the base of my stomach. I believe I never appreciated, till then, the poverty of the human machinery—for I still needed a hand or two to place elsewhere. Pen cannot describe how I was jolted up. Imagination cannot conceive how disjointed I was—how internally, externally and universally I was unsettled, mixed up and ruptured. There was a sympathetic crowd around me, though.

One elderly-looking comforter said:

"Stranger, you've been taken in. Everybody in this camp knows that horse. Any child, any Injun, could have told you that he'd buck; he is the very worst devil to buck on the continent of America. You hear me. I'm Curry. Old Curry. Old Abe Curry. And moreover, he is a simon-pure, out-and-out, genuine d—d Mexican plug, and an uncommon mean one at that, too. Why, you turnip, if you had laid low and kept dark, there's chances to buy an American horse for mighty little more than you paid for that bloody old foreign relic."

I gave no sign; but I made up my mind that if the auctioneer's brother's funeral took place while I was in the Territory I would postpone all other recreations and attend it.

After a gallop of sixteen miles the Californian youth and the Genuine Mexican Plug came tearing into town again, shedding foam-flakes like the spume-spray that drives before a typhoon, and, with one final skip over a wheelbarrow and a Chinaman, cast anchor in front of the "ranch."

Such panting and blowing! Such spreading and contracting of the red equine nostrils, and glaring of the wild equine eye! But was the imperial beast subjugated? Indeed he was not. His lordship the Speaker of the House thought he was, and mounted him to go down to the Capitol;

Every man who rides the Mexican plug ends up walking back.

but the first dash the creature made was over a pile of telegraph poles half as high as a church; and his time to the Capitol—one mile and three quarters—remains unbeaten to this day. But then he took an advantage—he left out the mile, and only did the three quarters. That is to say, he made a straight cut across lots, preferring fences and ditches to a crooked road; and when the Speaker got to the Capitol he said he had been in the air so much he felt as if he had made the trip on a comet.

In the evening the Speaker came home afoot for exercise, and got the Genuine towed back behind a quartz wagon. The next day I loaned the animal to the Clerk of the House to go down to the Dana silver mine, six miles, and he walked back for exercise, and got the horse towed. Everybody I loaned him to always walked back; they never could get enough exercise any other way. Still, I continued to loan him to anybody who was willing to borrow him, my idea being to get him crippled, and throw him on the borrower's hands, or killed, and make the borrower pay for him. But somehow nothing ever happened to him. He took chances that no other horse ever took and survived, but he always came out safe. It was his daily habit to try experiments that had always before been considered impossible, but he always got through. Sometimes he miscalculated a little, and did not get his rider through intact, but he always got through himself. Of course I had tried to sell him; but that was a stretch of simplicity which met with little sympathy. The auctioneer stormed up and down the streets on him for four days, dispersing the populace, interrupting business, and destroying children, and never got a bid—at least never any but the eighteen-dollar one he hired a notoriously substanceless bummer to make. The people only smiled pleasantly, and restrained their desire to buy, if they had any. Then the auctioneer brought in his bill, and I withdrew the horse from the market. We tried to trade him off at private vendue next, offering him at a sacrifice for second-hand tombstones, old iron, temperance tracts—any kind of property. But holders were stiff, and we retired from the market again. I never tried to ride the horse any more. Walking was good enough exercise for a man like me, that had nothing the matter with him except ruptures, internal injuries, and such things. Finally I tried to give him away. But it was a failure. Parties said earthquakes were handy enough on the Pacific coast—they did not wish to own one. As a last resort I offered him to the Governor for the use of the "Brigade." His face lit up eagerly at first, but toned down again, and he said the thing would be too palpable.

Just then the livery stable man brought in his bill for six weeks' keeping—stall-room for the horse, fifteen dollars; hay for the horse, two hundred and fifty! The Genuine Mexican Plug had eaten a ton of the article, and the man said he would have eaten a hundred if he had let him.

I will remark here, in all seriousness, that the regular price of hay during that year and a part of the next was really two hundred and fifty dollars a ton. During a part of the previous year it had sold at five hundred a ton, in gold, and during the winter before that there was such scarcity of the article that in several instances small quantities had brought eight hundred dollars a ton in coin! The consequence might be guessed without my telling it: peopled turned their stock loose to starve, and before the spring arrived Carson and Eagle valleys were almost literally carpeted with their carcases! Any old settler there will verify these statements.

I managed to pay the livery bill, and that same day I gave the Genuine Mexican Plug to a passing Arkansas emigrant whom fortune delivered into my hand. If this ever meets his eye, he will doubtless remember the donation.

Now whoever has had the luck to ride a real Mexican plug will recognize the animal depicted in this chapter, and hardly consider him exaggerated—but the uninitiated will feel justified in regarding his portrait as a fancy sketch, perhaps.

—*Roughing It* (1872), chapter 24

Much of Roughing It *is pure fiction, but we can be reasonably certain that the Mexican plug incident actually occurred because Mark Twain was fond of retelling the story. In the ninth chapter of* My Father, Mark Twain *(1931), his daughter Clara recalls that during his around-the-world lecture tour in 1895–1896, the horse story "never failed to bring bursts of laughter . . . that spread into uproars of mirth." She recalled her father's saying: "Well, that horse gave such a buck-jump at last that it sent me out of the saddle up and up—and up so high I came across birds I never saw before. I kept on going and just missed the top of a steeple. But when I got back the horse—was gone."*

Mark Twain also retold the Mexican plug story in a speech he gave in Bermuda in 1908. He recalled being so exhilarated by the picturesque sight of graceful horsemen flying through the town every day that he wished "I could try that great art some day, to fly through the town with incredible swiftness and disappear next minute in a cloud of dust. I got possessed with the passion and desire to become a horseman." His description of his first attempt to ride the Mexican plug in that speech is even more colorful than his original version in Roughing It.

When he [the horse] came out he interested himself in everything going on. He couldn't stand still. Wanted to be doing something right away. He just looked me over and appeared to be glad of my society. Some of the boys held him down by the head while the others held him to earth by the tail. I got on him. The minute I was in the saddle I was up in the air, and up and up and up. Came down and alighted in the saddle again. Up again and down again. He went through the maneuver until he was tired of it. I was ahead of him in that.

Finally, he stood on his hind legs, just on his toe nails, looking at the scenery. I had hold of him around the neck. He had no ears. I thought I would slide down and get down the back way. I was too late. He resumed the original performance and shot me in the air. I would not like to say how high I did go. It would sound like exaggeration. But really, I came across birds up there.

When I came down he was gone. I have not practiced any horsemanship since. It was a valuable lesson I learned. It meant a great deal to me. I have been able to avoid horsemanship ever since, and it has probably saved my life.

—speech in Hamilton, Bermuda, April 9, 1908

3

THE WORLD'S POOREST HORSEMAN?

Mark Twain's Mexican plug misadventure was not his only equine encounter in Nevada; others are related later in this book. For now, we jump ahead to his time in Hawaii, where he probably did more horseback riding than at any other period in his life. During the four months he spent on the islands in 1866, he rode horses almost everywhere he went. Those journeys were not always happy ones, but as this letter he wrote for a California newspaper reveals, they were filled with both memorable moments and unforgettable animals.

COMING HOME FROM PRISON

I am probably the most sensitive man in the kingdom of Hawaii to night—especially about sitting down in the presence of my betters. I have ridden fifteen or twenty miles on horseback since 5 p.m., and to tell the honest truth, I have a delicacy about sitting down at all. I am one of the poorest horsemen in the world, and I never mount a horse without experiencing a sort of dread that I may be setting out on that last mysterious journey which all of us must take sooner or later, and I never come back in safety from a horseback trip without thinking of my latter end for two or three days afterward. This same old regular devotional sentiment began just as soon as I sat down here five minutes ago.

An excursion to Diamond Head and the King's Cocoanut Grove was planned to-day—time, 4:30 p.m.—the party to consist of half a dozen gentlemen and three ladies. They all started at the appointed hour except myself. I was at the Government Prison, and got so interested in its examination that I did not notice how quickly the time was passing. Somebody remarked that it was twenty minutes past five o'clock, and that woke me up. It was a fortunate circumstance that Captain Phillips was there with his "turn-out," as he calls a top-buggy that Captain Cook brought here in 1778, and a horse that was here when Captain Cook came. Captain Phillips takes a just pride in his driving and in the speed of his horse, and to his passion for displaying them I owe it that we were only sixteen minutes coming from the prison to the American Hotel—a distance which has been estimated to be over half a mile. But it took some awful driving. The Captain's whip came down fast, and the blows started so much dust out of the horse's hide that during the last half of the journey we rode through an impenetrable fog, and ran by a pocket compass in the hands of Captain Fish, a whaler Captain of twenty-six years' experience, who sat there through that perilous voyage as self-possessed as if he had been on the euchre-deck of his own ship, and calmly said, "Port your helm-port," from time to time, and "Hold her a little free-steady—so-o," and "Luff—hard down to starboard!" and never once lost his presence of mind or betrayed the least anxiety by voice or manna. When we came to anchor at last, and Captain Phillips looked at his watch and said, "Sixteen minutes—I told you it was in her! that's ova three miles an hour!" I could see he felt entitled to a compliment, and so I said I had never seen lightning go like that horse. And I never had.

THE STEED OAHU

The landlord of the American said the party had been gone nearly an hour, but that he could give me my choice of several horses that could easily overtake them. I said, never mind—I preferred a safe horse to a fast one—I would like to have an excessively gentle horse—a horse with no spirit whatever—a lame one, if he had such a thing. Inside of five minutes I was mounted, and perfectly satisfied with my outfit. I had no time to label him "This is a horse," and so if the public took him for a sheep I cannot help it. I was satisfied, and that was the main thing. I could see that he had as many fine points as any man's horse, and I just hung my hat on one of them, behind the saddle, and swabbed the perspiration from my face and started. I named him after this island, "Oahu" (pronounced O-waw-hoo). The first gate he came to he started

The villainy of Oahu's nature came out again when he tried to climb over a stone wall.

in; I had neither whip nor spur, and so I simply argued the case with him. He firmly resisted argument, but ultimately yielded to insult and abuse. He backed out of that gate and steered for another one on the other side of the street. I triumphed by my former process. Within the next six hundred yards he crossed the street fourteen times and attempted thirteen gates, and in the meantime the tropical sun was beating down and threatening to cave the top of my head in, and I was literally dripping with perspiration and profanity. (I am only human and I was sorely aggravated. I shall behave better next time.) He quit the gate business after that and went along peaceably enough, but absorbed in meditation. I noticed this latter circumstance, and it soon began to fill me with the gravest apprehension. I said to myself, this malignant brute is planning some new outrage, some fresh deviltry or other—no horse ever thought over a subject so profoundly as this one is doing just for nothing. The more this thing preyed upon my mind the more uneasy I became, until at last the suspense became unbeatable and I dismounted to see if there was anything wild in his eye—for I had heard that the eye of this noblest of out domestic animals is very expressive. I cannot describe what a load of anxiety was lifted from my mind when I found that he was only asleep. I woke him up and started him into a faster walk, and then the inborn villainy of his nature came out again. He tried to climb over a stone wall, five or six feet high. I saw that I must apply force to this horse, and that I might as well begin first as last. I plucked a stout switch from a tamarind tree, and the moment he saw it, he gave in. He broke into a convulsive sort of a canter, which had three short steps in it and one long one, and reminded me alternately of the clattering shake of the great earth quake, and the sweeping plunging of the *Ajax* in a storm.

OUT OF PRISON, BUT IN THE STOCKS

And now it occurs to me that there can be no fitter occasion than the present to pronounce a fervent curse upon the man who invented the American saddle. There is no seat to speak of about it—one might as well sit in a shovel—and the stirrups are nothing but an ornamental nuisance. If I were to write down here all the abuse I expended on those stirrups, it would make a large book, even without pictures. Sometimes I got one foot so far through, that the stirrup partook of the nature of an anklet—sometimes both feet were through and I was handcuffed by the legs and some times my feet got clear out and left the stirrups wildly dangling about my shins. Even when I was in proper position and carefully balanced upon the balls of my feet, there was no comfort in it, on account of my nervous dread that they were going to slip one way or the other in a moment. But the subject is too exasperating to write about.

—letter to *Sacramento Union*, published April 21, 1866

Mark Twain repeated most of this letter in chapter 64 of Roughing It. *Perhaps significantly, the book omits the first paragraph's sentences about being a poor horseman and dreading what would become of him every time he mounted a horse.*

4

A RIDE TOO FAR

The preceding account of Mark Twain's long horseback ride in Hawaii was not the whole story. In this second letter to a Sacramento newspaper, he finishes describing the arduous ride and adds some curious observations about the steed Oahu.

I wandered along the sea beach on my steed Oahu around the base of the extinct crater of Leahi, or Diamond Head, and a quarter of a mile beyond the point I overtook the party of ladies and gentlemen and assumed my proper place—that is, in the rear—for the horse I ride always persists in remaining in the rear in spite of kicks, cuffs and curses. I was satisfied as long as I could keep Oahu within hailing distance of the cavalcade—I knew I could accomplish nothing better even if Oahu were Norfolk [a harness-racing breed] himself.

We went on—on—on—a great deal too far, I thought, for people who were unaccustomed to riding on horseback, and who must expect to suffer on the morrow if they indulged too freely in this sort of exercise. Finally we got to a point which we were expecting to go around in order to strike an easy road home; but we were too late; it was full tide and the sea had closed in on the shore. Young Henry McFarlane said he knew a nice, comfortable route over the hill—a short cut—and the crowd dropped into his wake. We climbed a hill a hundred and fifty feet high, and about as straight up and down as the side of a house, and as full of rough lava blocks as it could stick—not as wide, perhaps, as the broad road that leads to destruction, but nearly as dangerous to travel, and apparently leading in the same general direction. I felt for the ladies, but I had no time to speak any words of sympathy, by reason of my attention being so much occupied by Oahu. The place was so steep that at times he stood straight up on his tip-toes and clung by his forward toenails, with his back to the Pacific Ocean and his nose close to the moon—and thus situated we formed an equestrian picture which was as uncomfortable to me as it may have been picturesque to the spectators. You may think I was afraid, but I was not. I knew I could stay on him as long as his ears did not pull out.

COMING OUT A WINNER!

"We rode horseback all around the island of Hawaii (the crooked road making the distance two hundred miles), and enjoyed the journey very much. We were more than a week making the trip . . .

"In due course of time our journey came to an end at Kawaehae. . . . I made this horseback trip on a mule. I paid ten dollars for him at Kau (Kah-oo), added four to get him shod, rode him two hundred miles, and then sold him for fifteen dollars. I mark the circumstance with a white stone, . . . for up to that day and date it was the first strictly commercial transaction I had ever entered into, and come out winner."

—*Roughing It* (1872), chapter 76

It was a great relief to me to know that we were all safe and sound on the summit at last, because the sun was just disappearing in the waves, night was abroad in the land, candles and lamps were already twinkling in the distant town, and we gratefully reflected that Henry had saved us from having to go back around the rocky, sandy beach. But a new trouble arose while the party were admiring the rising moon and the cool, balmy night breeze, with its odor of countless flowers, for it was discovered that we had got into a place we could not get out of—we were apparently surrounded by precipices—our pilot's chart was at fault, and he could not extricate us, and so we had the prospect before us of either spending the night in the admired night-breeze, under the admired moon, or of clambering down the way we came, in the dark.

How ever, a Kanaka [native Hawaiian] came along presently and found a first-rate road for us down an almost imperceptible decline, and the party set out on a cheerful gallop again, and Oahu struck up his miraculous canter once more. The moon rose up, and flooded mountain and valley and ocean with silvery light, and I was not sorry we had lately been in trouble, because the consciousness of being safe again raised our spirits and made us more capable of enjoying the beautiful scene than we would have been otherwise. I never breathed such a soft, delicious atmosphere before, nor one freighted with such rich fragrance. A barber shop is nothing to it. . . .

The narrative then describes the excursionists exploring an ancient battlefield littered with human bones.

Oahu sits down to listen—but to what?

At this point the horse called Oahu deliberately sat down in the sand. Sat down to listen, I suppose. Never mind what he heard. I stopped apostrophising and convinced him that I was not a man to allow contempt of Court on the part of a horse. I broke the back bone of a Chief over his rump and set out to join the cavalcade again.

Very considerably fagged out we arrived in town at 9 o'clock at night, myself in the lead—for when my horse finally came to understand that he was homeward bound and hadn't far to go, he threw his legs wildly out before and behind him, depressed his head and laid his ears back, and flew by the admiring company like a telegram. In five minutes he was far away ahead of everybody.

—letter to *Sacramento Union*, published April 24, 1866

A TIMID "FRENCHMAN"

"I speak French with timidity and not flowing except when excited. When using that language I have often noticed that I have hardly ever been mistaken for a Frenchman, except by the horses. Never, I believe, by people."

—speech in Montreal, Canada, December 10, 1881

5

DIFFIDENCE ABOUT HORSES

It's not clear exactly when Mark Twain's next significant riding experiences occurred after he left the Far West for the last time in 1868. His travel book Following the Equator *recalls a moment during one of his visits to England in the early 1870s, when he declined an invitation to ride a horse in a fox hunt, feeling it would be safer to stay closer to the ground. This anecdote appears within his description of a chance meeting with an old friend, when he told the friend about a fox hunt he had once seen.*

"It was a quarter of a century ago—1873 or '74. I had an American friend in London named F., who was fond of hunting, and his friends the Blanks invited him and me to come out to a hunt and be their guests at their country place. In the morning the mounts were provided, but when I saw the horses I changed my mind and asked permission to walk. I had never seen an English hunter before, and it seemed to me that I could hunt a fox safer on the ground. I had always been diffident about horses, anyway, even those of the common altitudes, and I did not feel competent to hunt on a horse that went on stilts. So then Mrs. Blank came to my help and said I could go with her in the dog-cart and we would drive to a place she knew of, and there we should have a good glimpse of the hunt as it went by.

"When we got to that place I got out and went and leaned my elbows on a low stone wall which enclosed a turfy and beautiful great field with heavy wood on all its sides except ours. Mrs. Blank sat in the dog-cart fifty yards away, which was as near as she could get with the vehicle. I was full of interest, for I had never seen a fox-hunt. I waited, dreaming and imagining, in the deep stillness and impressive tranquillity which reigned in that retired spot. Presently, from away off in the forest on the left, a mellow bugle-note came floating; then all of a sudden a multitude of dogs burst out of that forest and went tearing by and disappeared in the forest on the right; there was a pause, and then a cloud of horsemen in black caps and crimson coats plunged out of the left-hand forest and went flaming across the field like a prairie-fire, a stirring sight to see. There was one man ahead of the rest, and he came spurring straight at me. He was fiercely excited. It was fine to see him ride; he was a master horseman. He came like a storm till he was within seven feet of me, where I was leaning on the wall, then he stood his horse straight up in the air on his hind toe-nails, and shouted like a demon:

"'Which way'd the fox go?'

"I didn't much like the tone, but I did not let on; for he was excited, you know. But I was calm; so I said softly, and without acrimony:

Mark Twain was diffident about riding horses on stilts.

"'*Which* fox?'

"It seemed to anger him. I don't know why; and he thundered out:

"'*Which* fox? Why, *the* fox! Which way did the *fox* go?'

"I said, with great gentleness—even argumentatively:

"'If you could be a little more definite—a little less vague—because I am a stranger, and there are many foxes, as you will know even better than I, and unless I know which one it is that you desire to identify, and—'

"'You're certainly the damnedest idiot that has escaped in a thousand years!' and he snatched his great horse around as easily as I would snatch a cat, and was away like a hurricane. A very excitable man."

—*Following the Equator* (1897), chapter 20

"There was that rare thing, novelty, about it; it was a fresh, new, exhilarating sensation, this donkey riding, and worth a hundred worn and threadbare home pleasures."

PART II

HAPPY TRAILS

Mark Twain's interactions with horses and their kin were not always uncomfortable. He had many pleasurable experiences with them and especially enjoyed riding donkeys, which he appreciated because they were built closer to the ground than horses. He also derived pleasure from watching other unskilled riders struggling with their mounts; that is particularly evident in his description of the "ragged and uncouth procession" with which he rode across the Isthmus of Central America. This section also contains samples of pleasant riding experiences in Hawaii, Europe, and Asia Minor—but note, Mark Twain himself is not always the rider whose reminiscences are pleasant.

During the four months that Mark Twain spent in Hawaii in 1866, he probably did more horseback riding than at any other period of his life.

6

THE HAWAIIAN LOVE OF HORSES

Mark Twain began his career as a professional lecturer in San Francisco in October 1866. Having just returned from his sojourn in Hawaii (then known to Americans as the Sandwich Islands), it was natural for him to lecture about the Native Hawaiians, whom he generally called "Kanakas"—a somewhat disrespectful term for Polynesians and other South Sea islanders. Not surprisingly, his Hawaiian lectures have a great deal to say about horses.

Kanakas are fond of horses, and they have got plenty of them. They seldom walk anywhere; they nearly always ride. Whenever you see a lot of men and women at work in a sugar plantation, you will see as many horses hitched at hand for them to ride a quarter of a mile home on. These horses are worth on an average about seven dollars and a half apiece (you can often buy them for less, though), and they have to pay a government tax of a dollar a head on them. But that doesn't matter. A Kanaka with an income of fifty dollars a year will keep half a dozen horses, if it breaks him. And he is as unkind and as unmerciful to his horse as he is disgustingly fond of his puppy. His horse is seldom well fed and is always hard ridden. And they can make a horse go when a white man can't. If there is any of that capacity in a horse the Kanaka will get it out. I once rode over a mountain in Mani [Maui?] with a white man whose horse was so lean and spiritless and worthless that he could not be persuaded or spurred out of a walk, and he kept going to sleep, besides—at least he seemed to. But the man said that when he got to Maaleo Bay he would find one of his own horses there—a blooded animal that could outstrip the wind. He got his blooded animal, and gave the slow horse to a Kanaka boy and told him to follow. Then he put his blooded steed to his utmost speed to show him off. But the Kanaka, without spur or whip, or scarcely any appearance of urging, sailed by us on the old plug, and stayed ahead, and in eight miles he beat us out of sight. I never could understand how those savages managed to make those wretched horses travel so. They are wild, free riders, and perfectly at home in the saddle—they call it a saddle, a little vile English spoon of a thing with a girth that never is tight enough to touch the horse and sometimes without any girth at all. With their loose ideas, they never cinch a Californian's horse tight enough to suit him.

Hawaiian women all ride horses, and they ride well and gracefully.

When a Kanaka rides through the country, he stops fifteen or twenty minutes at every single cabin he comes to, and has a chat. Consequently their horses early acquire the inveterate habit of stopping, and they cannot be cured of it. If you attempt to keep them in the road and go on about your business, they grow frantic and kick up and charge around fiercely, and finally take the bits in their mouths and carry you to the cabin by main force. I rode Kanaka horses nearly altogether. When I made the tour of that pleasant country I hadn't any business at any of the roadside cabins, but I stopped at them all. The horses wanted to stop, and I had to put up with it. That is how I happen to have such an intimate knowledge of the country and the people.

The Kanaka women all ride, and ride well and gracefully. They ride as women *should* ride—astride. To ride sidewise tires the horse, makes his back sore and his footing insecure, and endangers the life of the rider. A sidesaddle is always turning and spilling its precious freight into the mud or on the rocks and bruising the limbs or breaking the neck of the same. For a woman to ride sidewise is to do an awkward, ungainly, absurd, and to the last degree foolish and perilous thing.

—"The Sandwich Islands," *Mark Twain's Speeches*, 2nd ed. (1923)

BROWN'S PRIVATE PROCESSION

"[Brown] had to take his party horseback, and in order to keep them together amid the confusion of the procession, he tied his five mules together, end to end, and marched in single file—the forward horse's tail made fast to the next one's nose, and so on. He rode the leading horse himself, with the baby in his arms; Mrs. B. and the two boys came next, and the servant girl brought up the rear. It was a solemnly comical spectacle. Everything went well, though."

—undated letter to *Alta California*, 1867

7

A RAGGED AND UNCOUTH PROCESSION

In late 1866, after Mark Twain ended his long residence in the Far West, he sailed from San Francisco down the Pacific Coast to Nicaragua, where he crossed the isthmus and resumed his sea voyage to the East. More than four hundred passengers crossed the isthmus with him. Most rode mules and horses; the rest traveled in rickety wheeled conveyances. Few of them were competent riders; much of their gear was worn and decayed, and traversing mountains and tropical forests was inherently difficult and perilous. The result was the "wildest, raggedest and most uncouth procession" Mark Twain ever witnessed. Amazingly, everyone appears to have survived the crossing—which he found highly entertaining.

Greytown, January 1st [1867].—While we lay all night at San Juan, the baggage was sent ashore in lighters, and next morning we departed ourselves. We found San Juan to consist of a few tumble-down frame shanties—they call them hotels—nestling among green verdure and overshadowed by picturesque little hills. The spot where we landed was crowded with horses, mules, ambulances and half-clad yellow natives, with bowie-knives two feet long, and as broad as your hand, strapped to their waists. I thought these barefooted scoundrels were soldiers, but no, they were merely citizens in civil life. Here and there on the beach moved a soiled and ragged white woman, to whom the sight of our ship must have been as a vision of Paradise; for here a vast ship-load of passengers had been kept in exile for fifteen days through the wretched incompetency of one man—the Company's agent on the Isthmus. He had sent a steamer empty to San Francisco, when he knew well that this multitude of people were due at Greytown. They will finish their journey, now, in our ship.

Our party of eight—we had made it up the night before—being the first boat-load to leave the ship, was entitled to the first choice of the ambulances, or the equestrian accommodations that were to convey us the twelve miles we must go by land between San Juan and Virgin Bay, on Lake Nicaragua. Some of the saddle-horses and mules—many of them, in fact—looked very well; but if there was any choice between the ambulances, or especially between the miraculous scarecrows that were to haul them, it was hardly perceptible. You never saw such harness in your life, nor such mules, nor such drivers. They were funny individually and funny in combination. Except the ghastly sores on the animals' backs, where the crazy harness had chafed, and scraped, and scarified—that part of it would move anybody's pity for the poor things.

We climbed into one of the largest of the faded red ambulances (mud wagons we call them in the mountains), with four little sore-backed rabbits hitched to it, and cleared for Virgin Bay. The driver commenced by beating and banging his team and cursing them like a furious maniac, in bad Spanish, and he kept it up all through that twelve-mile journey of three hours and a half, over a hard, level, beautiful road. We envied the people who were not crippled and could ride horseback.

But we clattered along pretty lively, and were a jolly party. The first thing the ladies noticed as we lost sight of the sea, and wound in among an overshadowing growth of dewy vines and forest trees, was a "dear, dear little baby—oh, see the darling!"—a vile, distempered, mud-colored native brat, making dirt-pies in front of an isolated cabin; and the first thing the men noticed was—was—but they could not make it out; a guide board perhaps, or a cross, or the modest grave-stone of some ill fated stranger. But it was none of these. When we drew nearer it turned out to be a sign nailed to a tree, and it said "Try Ward's shirts!" . . .

THE PROCESSION UNDER WAY

The bright, fresh green on every hand, the delicious softness and coolness of the air (it had just showered a little before we started), the interest of unknown birds and flowers and trees, the delightful new sensation of the bumping and rattling of the ambulance—everything so cheery and lively, as compared with our old dull monotony and shoreless sea on board the ship—wrought our party up to a pitch of joyous animation and enthusiasm that I would have thought impossible with such dry old sticks. . . .

MASQUERADING ON THE ROAD

Our four hundred passengers on horseback, muleback, and in four-mule ambulances, formed the wildest, raggedest and most uncouth procession I ever saw. It reminded me of the fantastic masquerading pageants

The hundreds of passengers on horseback and muleback and carts formed the wildest, raggedest, and most uncouth procession Mark Twain ever saw.

they used to get up on the Fourth of July in the Western States, or on Mardigras Day in New Orleans. The steerage passengers travelled on muleback, chiefly, with coats, oil-skin carpet sacks, and blankets dangling around their saddles. Some of the saddles were new and good, but others were in all possible stages of mutilation and decay. There were not a dozen good riders in the two hundred and fifty that went on horseback, but every man seemed to consider that inasmuch as the animals belonged to "the Company," it was a stern duty to ride them to death, if possible, and they tried hard to do it. Such racing and yelling, and beating and banging and spurring, and such bouncing of blanket bundles, and flapping and fluttering of coat-tails, and such frantic scampering of the multitude of mules, and bobbing up and down of the long column of men, and rearing and charging of struggling ambulances in their midst, I never saw before, and I never enjoyed anything so much.

—undated letter to *Alta California*, published May 15, 1867

8

A NEW AND EXHILARATING SENSATION

In 1867, Mark Twain sailed to Europe and the Middle East aboard the steamship Quaker City *on one of the world's first tourist cruises. During that trip, he rode donkeys, mules, and horses in several countries and described colorful experiences in travel letters to American newspapers that he later revised in his first great travel book,* The Innocents Abroad. *His first stop on the voyage was at one of the islands in Portugal's Azores archipelago. There he found donkey riding a pleasant change from the challenges of horseback riding in Hawaii.*

I think the Azores must be very little known in America. Out of our whole ship's company there was not a solitary individual who knew any thing whatever about them. . . .

As we came down through the town, we encountered a squad of little donkeys ready saddled for use. The saddles were peculiar, to say the least. They consisted of a sort of saw-buck, with a small mattress on it, and this furniture covered about half the donkey. There were no stirrups, but really such supports were not needed—to use such a saddle was the next thing to riding a dinner table—there was ample support clear out to one's knee joints. A pack of ragged Portuguese muleteers crowded around us, offering their beasts at half a dollar an hour—more rascality to the stranger, for the market price is sixteen cents. Half a dozen of us mounted the ungainly affairs, and submitted to the indignity

Riding a donkey had that rare thing, novelty, about it.

of making a ridiculous spectacle of ourselves through the principal streets of a town of 10,000 inhabitants.

We started. It was not a trot, a gallop, or a canter, but a stampede, and made up of all possible or conceivable gaits. No spurs were necessary. There was a muleteer to every donkey and a dozen volunteers beside, and they banged the donkeys with their goad-sticks, and pricked them with their spikes, and shouted something that sounded like "Sekki-yah!" and kept up a din and a racket that was worse than Bedlam itself. These rascals were all on foot, but no matter, they were always up to time—they can outrun and outlast a donkey. Altogether ours was a lively and a picturesque procession, and drew crowded audiences to the balconies wherever we went.

Blucher could do nothing at all with his donkey. The beast scampered zigzag across the road and the others ran into him; he scraped Blucher against carts and the corners of houses; the road was fenced in with high stone walls, and the donkey gave him a polishing first on one side and then on the other, but never once took the middle; he finally came to the house he was born in and darted into the parlor, scraping Blucher off at the doorway. After remounting, Blucher said to the muleteer, "Now, that's enough, you know; you go slow here-after." But the fellow knew no English and did not understand, so he simply said, "Sekki-yah!" and the donkey was off again like a shot. He turned a corner suddenly, and Blucher went over his head. And, to speak truly, every mule stumbled over the two, and the whole cavalcade was piled up in a heap. No harm done. A fall from one of those donkeys is of little more consequence than rolling off a sofa. The donkeys all stood still after the catastrophe, and waited for their dismembered saddles to be patched up and put on by the noisy muleteers. Blucher was pretty angry, and wanted to swear, but every time he opened his mouth his animal did so also, and let off a series of brays that drowned all other sounds.

It was fun, skurrying around the breezy hills and through the beautiful canons. There was that rare thing, novelty, about it; it was a fresh, new, exhilarating sensation, this donkey riding, and worth a hundred worn and threadbare home pleasures.

The roads were a wonder, and well they might be. Here was an island with only a handful of people in it—25,000—and yet such fine roads do not exist in the United States outside of Central Park. Every where you go, in any direction, you find either a hard, smooth, level thoroughfare, just sprinkled with black lava sand, and bordered with little gutters neatly paved with small smooth pebbles, or compactly paved ones like Broadway. They talk much of the Russ pavement in New York, and call it a new invention—yet here they have been using it in this remote little isle of the sea for two hundred years! Every street in Horta is handsomely paved with the heavy Russ blocks, and the surface is neat and true as a floor—not marred by holes like Broadway. And every road is fenced in by tall, solid lava walls, which will last a thousand years in this land where frost is unknown. They are very thick, and are often plastered and whitewashed, and capped with projecting slabs of cut stone. Trees from gardens above hang their swaying tendrils down, and contrast their bright green with the whitewash or the black lava of the walls, and make them beautiful. The trees and vines stretch across these narrow roadways sometimes, and so shut out the sun that you seem to be riding through a tunnel. The pavements, the roads, and the bridges are all government work.

The bridges are of a single span—a single arch—of cut stone, without a support, and paved on top with flags of lava and ornamental pebble work. Every where are walls, walls, walls,—and all of them tasteful and handsome—and eternally substantial; and every where are those marvelous pavements, so neat, so smooth, and so indestructible. And if ever roads and streets, and the outsides of houses, were perfectly free from any sign or semblance of dirt, or dust, or mud, or uncleanliness of any kind, it is Horta, it is Fayal. The lower classes of the people, in their persons and their domicil[e]s, are not clean—but there it stops—the town and the island are miracles of cleanliness.

After Blucher lost control of his donkey, others ran into it, until there was a general pileup.

We arrived home again finally, after a ten-mile excursion, and the irrepressible muleteers scampered at our heels through the main street, goading the donkeys, shouting the everlasting "Sekki-yah," and singing "John Brown's Body" in ruinous English.

When we were dismounted and it came to settling, the shouting and jawing, and swearing and quarreling among the muleteers and with us, was nearly deafening. One fellow would demand a dollar an hour for the use of his donkey; another claimed half a dollar for pricking him up, another a quarter for helping in that service, and about fourteen guides presented bills for showing us the way through the town and its environs; and every vagrant of them was more vociferous, and more vehement, and more frantic in gesture than his neighbor. We paid one guide, and paid for one muleteer to each donkey.

—*The Innocents Abroad* (1869), chapter 6

Here it should be mentioned that the name of Mark Twain's inept and often gauche traveling companion, Blucher, was not that of a real person. Mark Twain based some of Blucher's mishaps on those of fellow Quaker City *passengers and used him as a comic foil in his letters to the* New York Tribune. *Blucher—or a close cousin—also appeared as Mr. Brown in letters Mark Twain wrote to the San Francisco* Alta California. *Blucher and Brown both appear in other perilous adventures.*

THE JACKASS

"There is no character, howsoever good and fine, but it can be destroyed by ridicule, howsoever poor and witless. Observe the ass, for instance: his character is about perfect, he is the choicest spirit among all the humbler animals, yet see what ridicule has brought him to. Instead of feeling complimented when we are called an ass, we are left in doubt."

—Pudd'nhead Wilson's Calendar, in *Pudd'nhead Wilson* (1894)

9

DOWNSIZED DONKEYS

We have just seen how much Mark Twain enjoyed riding a donkey in the Azores. He had a similar riding experience later when he toured the famed ruins of Ephesus in Asia Minor. He was among about sixty Quaker City *passengers (whom he teasingly called "pilgrims") and American naval officers who rode a special train from the port of Smyrna to Ephesus, where they mounted donkeys for the tour. Many of the travelers were a little too big, and most of the donkeys were a little too small, but those disparities didn't spoil the fun.*

This has been a stirring day. The Superintendent of the railway put a train at our disposal, and did us the further kindness of accompanying us to Ephesus and giving to us his watchful care. We brought sixty scarcely perceptible donkeys in the freight cars, for we had much ground to go over. We have seen some of the most grotesque costumes, along the line of the railroad, that can be imagined. I am glad that no possible combination of words could describe them, for I might then be foolish enough to attempt it.

At ancient Ayassalook, in the midst of a forbidding desert, we came upon long lines of ruined aqueducts, and other remnants of architectural grandeur, that told us plainly enough we were nearing what had been a metropolis, once. We left the train and mounted the donkeys, along with our invited guests—pleasant young gentlemen from the officers' list of an American man-of-war.

The little donkeys had saddles upon them which were made very high in order that the rider's feet might not drag the ground. The preventative did not work well in the cases of our tallest pilgrims, however. There were no bridles—nothing but a single rope, tied to the bit. It was purely ornamental, for the donkey cared nothing for it. If he were drifting to starboard, you might put your helm down hard the other way, if it were any satisfaction to you to do it, but he would continue to drift to starboard all the same. There was only one process which could be depended on, and that was to get down and lift his rear around until his head pointed in the right direction, or take him under your arm and carry him to a part of the road which he could not get out of without climbing. The sun flamed down as hot as a furnace, and neck-scarfs, veils and umbrellas seemed hardly any protection; they served only to make the long procession look more than ever fantastic—for be it known the

Riding a little donkey at Ephesus.

ladies were all riding astride because they could not stay on the shapeless saddles sidewise, the men were perspiring and out of temper, their feet were banging against the rocks, the donkeys were capering in every direction but the right one and being belabored with clubs for it, and every now and then a broad umbrella would suddenly go down out of the cavalcade, announcing to all that one more pilgrim had bitten the dust. It was a wilder picture than those solitudes had seen for many a day. No donkeys ever existed that were as hard to navigate as these, I think, or that had so many vile, exasperating instincts. Occasionally we grew so tired and breathless with fighting them that we had to desist,—and immediately the donkey would come down to a deliberate walk. This, with the fatigue, and the sun, would put a man asleep; and as soon as the man was asleep, the donkey would lie down. My donkey shall never see his boyhood's home again. He has lain down once too often. He must die.

We all stood in the vast theatre of ancient Ephesus,—the stone-benched amphitheatre I mean—and had our picture taken. We looked as proper there as we would look any where, I suppose. We do not embellish the general desolation of a desert much. We add what dignity we can to a stately ruin with our green umbrellas and jackasses, but it is little. However, we mean well.

—*The Innocents Abroad* (1869), chapter 40

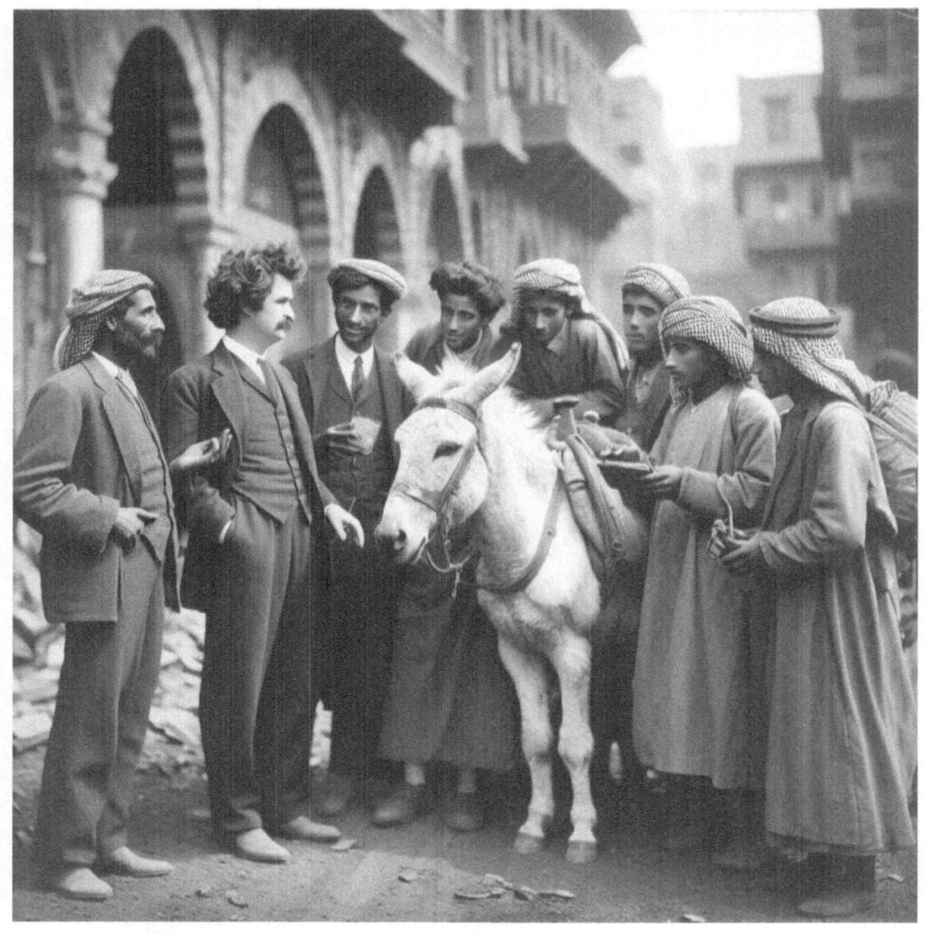

"Any where else we would have been assailed by a clamorous army of donkey-drivers, guides, peddlers and beggars."

PART III

HORSE TRADERS

Is there any class of entrepreneurship more closely associated with shrewdness and double-dealing than horse trading? As Wikipedia points out, "Due to the difficulties in evaluating the merits of a horse offered for sale, the sale of horses offered great opportunities for dishonesty." Mark Twain would certainly second that view. Almost everything he says about his own dealings with horse sellers emphasizes the latters' shady morals—from the time he bought his first horse (the genuine Mexican plug) in Nevada, through his later travels in Europe and the Middle East. In this section, we meet shifty horse traders in Hawaii, the Holy Land, and Egypt. Horse trading is also closely associated with the concept of "trading up": that is, trading an object for something of greater value and then trading that object for something more valuable still and so on. The final chapter here tells the story of a man who gained notoriety for trading down.

PUPPY LOVE

"[Hawaiians] love these puppies better than they love one another—better than their children or their religion. . . . Men and women carry these dogs in their arms, always. If they have got to walk a mile, the dog must be carried. . . . When the woman rides on horseback, she often carries the puppy in front of her on the horse; and when the man rides—they nearly always go in a keen gallop—the puppy stands up behind the saddle, 'thortships,' as a sailor would say, and sways gently to and fro to the motion of the horse. No danger of its falling; it is educated to ride thus from earliest puppyhood."

—"Sandwich Islands" lecture, October 2, 1866

10

SHREWD HAWAIIANS

Of all the horse traders with whom Mark Twain dealt during his travels, Native Hawaiians ("Kanakas") impressed him the most. Although he regarded Hawaiians as generally honest and averse to stealing, he saw something in them that made it impossible for them to do anything but lie when it came to dealing in horses. As has been pointed out, selling horses offers great opportunities for dishonesty. It may be a calumny to say so, but Mark Twain meant it in one of his speeches when he said Hawaiians "will lie for a dollar when they could get a dollar and a half for telling the truth."

This is a good time to drop in a paragraph of information. There is no regular livery stable in Honolulu, or, indeed, in any part of the kingdom of Hawaii; therefore unless you are acquainted with wealthy residents (who all have good horses), you must hire animals of the wretchedest description from the Kanakas. Any horse you hire, even though it be from a white man, is not often of much account, because it will be brought in for you from some ranch, and has necessarily been leading a hard life. If the Kanakas who have been caring for him (inveterate riders they are) have not ridden him half to death every day themselves, you can depend upon it they have been doing the same thing by proxy, by clandestinely hiring him out. At least, so I am informed. The result is, that no horse has a chance to eat, drink, rest, recuperate, or look well or feel well, and so strangers go about the Islands mounted as I was to-day.

In hiring a horse from a Kanaka, you must have all your eyes about you, because you can rest satisfied that you are dealing with as shrewd a rascal as ever patronized a penitentiary. You may leave your door open and your trunk unlocked as long as you please, and he will not meddle with your property; he has no important vices and no inclination to commit robbery on a large scale; but if he can get ahead of you in the horse business, he will take a genuine delight in doing it. This trait is characteristic of horse jockeys, the world over, is it not? He will overcharge you if he can; he will hire you a fine-looking horse at night (anybody's—maybe the King's, if the royal steed be in convenient view), and bring you the mate to my Oahu in the morning, and contend that it is the same animal. If you raise a row, he will get out by saying it was not himself who made the bargain with you, but his brother, "who went out in the country this morning." They have always got a "brother" to shift the responsibility upon. A victim said to one of these fellows one day:

Negotiating with a Hawaiian.

"But I know I hired the horse of you, because I noticed that scar on your cheek."

The reply was not bad: "Oh, yes—yes—my brother all same—we twins!"

A friend of mine, J. Smith, hired a horse yesterday, the Kanaka warranting him to be in excellent condition. Smith had a saddle and blanket of his own, and he ordered the Kanaka to put these on the horse. The Kanaka protested that he was perfectly willing to trust the gentleman with the saddle that was already on the animal, but Smith refused to use it. The change was made; then Smith noticed that the Kanaka had only changed the saddles, and had left the original blanket on the horse; he said he forgot to change the blankets, and so, to cut the bother short, Smith mounted and rode away. The horse went lame a mile from town, and afterward got to cutting up some extraordinary capers. Smith got down and took off the saddle, but the blanket stuck fast to the horse—glued to a procession of raw places. The Kanaka's mysterious conduct stood explained.

Another friend of mine bought a pretty good horse from a native, a day or two ago, after a tolerably thorough examination of the animal. He discovered to-day that the horse was as blind as a bat, in one eye. He meant to have examined that eye, and came home with a general notion that he had done it; but he remembers now that every time he made the attempt his attention was called to something else by his victimizer.

One more yarn, and then I will pass to something else. I am informed that when Leland was here, he bought a pair of very respectable-looking match horses from a native. They were in a little stable with a partition through the middle of it—one horse in each apartment. Leland examined one of them critically through a window (the Kanaka's "brother" having gone to the country with the key), and then went around the house and examined the other through a window on the other side. He said it was the neatest match he had ever seen, and paid for the horses on the spot. Whereupon the Kanaka departed to join his brother in the country. The scoundrel had shamefully swindled Leland. There was only one "match" horse, and he had examined his starboard side through one window and his port side through another! I decline to believe this story, but I give it because it is worth something as a fanciful illustration of a fixed fact—namely, that the Kanaka horse-jockey is fertile in invention and elastic in conscience.

HONOLULU PRICES FOR HORSEFLESH

You can buy a pretty good horse for forty or fifty dollars, and a good enough horse for all practical purposes for two dollars and a half. I estimate "Oahu" to be worth somewhere in the neighborhood of thirty-five cents. A good deal better animal than he is was sold here day before yesterday for a dollar and six bits, and sold again to-day for two dollars and twenty-five cents; Brown bought a handsome and lively little pony yesterday for ten dollars; and about the best common horse on the island (and he is a really good one) sold yesterday, with good Mexican saddle and bridle, for seventy dollars—a horse which is well and widely known, and greatly respected for his speed, good disposition and everlasting bottom. You give your horse a little grain once a day; it comes from San Francisco, and is worth about two cents a pound; and you give him as much hay as he wants; it is cut and brought to the market by natives, and is not very good; it is baled into long, round bundles, about the size of a large man; one of them is stuck by the middle on each end of a six-foot pole, and the Kanaka shoulders the pole and walks about the streets between the upright bales in search of customers. These hay bales, thus carried, have a general resemblance to a colossal capital H.

The hay-bundles cost twenty-five cents apiece, and one will last a horse about a day. You can get a horse for a song, a week's hay for another song, and you can turn your animal loose among the luxuriant grass in your neighbor's broad front yard without a song at all—you do it at midnight, and stable the beast again before morning. You have been at no expense thus far, but when you come to buy a saddle and bridle they will cost you from twenty to thirty-five dollars. You can hire a horse, saddle and bridle at from seven to ten dollars a week, and the owner will take care of them at his own expense.

—March 1866 letter to *Sacramento Union*, published April 21, 1866

Examining the horse through a window.

MEASURING DISTANCES

"All distances in the East are measured by hours, not miles. A good horse will walk three miles an hour over nearly any kind of a road; therefore, an hour here always stands for three miles. . . . I cannot be positive about it, but I think that there, when a man orders a pair of pantaloons, he says he wants them a quarter of a minute in the legs and nine seconds around the waist"

—*The Innocents Abroad* (1869), chapter 50

11

A RECKLESS LITTLE MULE

This anecdote concerning the big island of Hawaii reacquaints us with the imaginary traveling companion whom Mark Twain called Brown. Brown may not have been real, but the journey this passage describes almost certainly was real. It also contains another example of Native Hawaiian horse-trading duplicity and offers a surprising opinion of mules.

Brown bought a horse from a native at Waiohinu for twelve dollars, but happening to think of the horse-jockeying propensities of the race, he removed the saddle and found that the creature needed "half-soling," as he expressed it. Recent hard riding had polished most of the hide off his back. He bought another and the animal went dead lame before we got to the great volcano, forty miles away. I bought a reckless little mule for fifteen dollars, and I wish I had him yet. One mule is worth a dozen horses for a mountain journey in the Islands.

The first eighteen miles of the road lay mostly down by the sea, and was pretty well sprinkled with native houses. The animals stopped at all of them—a habit they had early acquired; natives stop a few minutes at every shanty they come to, to swap gossip, and we were forced to do likewise—but we did it under protest.

Brown's horse jogged along well enough for 16 or 17 miles, but then he came down to a walk and refused to improve on it. We had to stop and intrude upon a gentleman who was not expecting us, and who I thought did not want us, either, but he entertained us handsomely, nevertheless, and has my hearty thanks for his kindness.

—June 1866 letter to *Sacramento Daily Union*,
published October 25, 1866

Riding a mule in the islands.

12

A HARD LOT IN LEBANON

A little more than a year after leaving Hawaii, Mark Twain arrived in Beirut (the future capital of Lebanon), where he and seven other passengers from the Quaker City *hired a guide (dragoman) to organize a cross-country expedition through the Holy Land before rejoining the ship in Palestine. Their next step was to select the steeds they would ride on the expedition. The Beirut horse dealers were apparently not Native Hawaiians, but the animals they offered sound like they may have come from the islands. (We meet some of these horses again later.)*

At the appointed time our business committee reported, and said all things were in readiness—that we were to start to-day, with horses, pack animals, and tents, and go to Baalbec, Damascus, the Sea of Tiberias, and thence southward by the way of the scene of Jacob's Dream and other notable Bible localities to Jerusalem—from thence probably to the Dead Sea, but possibly not—and then strike for the ocean and rejoin the ship three or four weeks hence at Joppa [Jaffa, later part of Tel Aviv]; terms, five dollars a day apiece, in gold, and every thing to be furnished by the dragoman. They said we would live as well as at a hotel. I had read something like that before, and did not shame my judgment by believing a word of it. I said nothing, however, but packed up a blanket and a shawl to sleep in, pipes and tobacco, two or three woollen shirts, a portfolio, a guide-book, and a Bible. I also took along a towel and a cake of soap, to inspire respect in the Arabs, who would take me for a king in disguise.

Selecting horses in Beirut.

We were to select our horses at 3 p.m. At that hour Abraham, the dragoman, marshaled them before us. With all solemnity I set it down here, that those horses were the hardest lot I ever did come across, and their accoutrements were in exquisite keeping with their style. One brute had an eye out; another had his tail sawed off close, like a rabbit, and was proud of it; another had a bony ridge running from his neck to his tail, like one of those ruined aqueducts one sees about Rome, and had a neck on him like a bowsprit; they all limped, and had sore backs, and likewise raw places and old scales scattered about their persons like brass nails in a hair trunk; their gaits were marvelous to contemplate, and replete with variety—under way the procession looked like a fleet in a storm. It was fearful. Blucher shook his head and said:

"That dragon is going to get himself into trouble fetching these old crates out of the hospital the way they are, unless he has got a permit."

I said nothing. The display was exactly according to the guide-book, and were we not traveling by the guide-book? I selected a certain horse because I thought I saw him shy, and I thought that a horse that had spirit enough to shy was not to be despised.

At 6 o'clock p.m., we came to a halt here on the breezy summit of a shapely mountain overlooking the sea, and the handsome valley where dwelt some of those enterprising Phoenicians of ancient times we read so much about; all around us are what were once the dominions of Hiram, King of Tyre, who furnished timber from the cedars of these L[e]banon hills to build portions of King Solomon's Temple with.

Shortly after six, our pack train arrived. I had not seen it before, and a good right I had to be astonished. We had nineteen serving men and twenty-six pack mules! It was a perfect caravan. It looked like one, too, as it wound among the rocks. I wondered what in the very mischief we wanted with such a vast turn-out as that, for eight men. I wondered awhile, but soon I began to long for a tin plate, and some bacon and beans. I had camped out many and many a time before, and knew just what was coming. I went off, without waiting for serving men, and unsaddled my horse, and washed such portions of his ribs and his spine as projected through his hide, and when I came back, behold five stately circus tents were up—tents that were brilliant, within, with blue, and gold, and crimson, and all manner of splendid adornment! I was speechless. Then they brought eight little iron bedsteads, and set them up in the tents; they put a soft mattress and pillows and good blankets and two snow-white sheets on each bed. Next, they rigged a table about the centre-pole, and on it placed pewter pitchers, basins, soap, and the whitest of towels—one set for each man; they pointed to pockets in the tent, and said we could put our small trifles in them for convenience, and if we needed pins or such things, they were sticking every where. Then came the finishing touch—they spread carpets on the floor! I simply said, "If you call this camping out, all right—but it isn't the style I am used to; my little baggage that I brought along is at a discount."

—*The Innocents Abroad* (1869), chapter 41

The full-dressed tourist in the Holy Land.

13

THE OMNIBUSES OF EGYPT

After rejoining the Quaker City *in Palestine, the travelers moved on to Egypt—where Mark Twain encountered a new kind of "horse trading" and did more donkey riding.*

When we reached the pier we found an army of Egyptian boys with donkeys no larger than themselves, waiting for passengers—for donkeys are the omnibuses of Egypt. We preferred to walk, but we could not have our own way. The boys crowded about us, clamored around us, and slewed their donkeys exactly across our path, no matter which way we turned. They were good-natured rascals, and so were the donkeys. We mounted, and the boys ran behind us and kept the donkeys in a furious gallop, as is the fashion at Damascus. I believe I would rather ride a donkey than any beast in the world. He goes briskly, he puts on no airs, he is docile, though opinionated. Satan himself could not scare him, and he is convenient—very convenient. When you are tired riding you can rest your feet on the ground and let him gallop from under you.

—*The Innocents Abroad* (1869), chapter 57

The donkeys were even smaller than the Egyptian boys hiring them out.

14

THE MAN WHO PUT UP AT GADSBY'S

This isn't exactly a horse-trading tale. It concerns a man whose shrinking wherewithal forces him gradually to sell off his horses, carriages, and gear as he waits at a Washington, DC, hotel, seemingly forever, to settle a claim against the federal government. Mark Twain originally wrote the story as a parody about government inefficiency in 1868, while working as a newspaper correspondent in Washington; the version here he revised in 1880. His narrator, Riley, is a fellow correspondent who is telling a cautionary tale to a man who has just arrived and expects to be promptly appointed San Francisco's postmaster and be on his way home the next day.

"Have you ever heard about that man who put up at Gadsby's, once? . . . But I see you haven't."

He backed Mr. Lykins against an iron fence, buttonholed him, fastened him with his eye, like the Ancient Mariner, and proceeded to unfold his narrative as placidly and peacefully as if we were all stretched comfortably in a blossomy summer meadow instead of being persecuted by a wintry midnight tempest:

"I will tell you about that man. It was in Jackson's time. Gadsby's was the principal hotel, then. Well, this man arrived from Tennessee about nine o'clock, one morning, with a black coachman and a splendid four-horse carriage and an elegant dog, which he was evidently fond and proud of; he drove up before Gadsby's, and the clerk and the landlord

COULDN'T WAIT.

DIDN'T CARE FOR STYLE.

A PAIR BETTER THAN FOUR.

TWO WASN'T NECESSARY.

JUST THE TRICK.

GOING TO MAKE THEM STARE.

NOT THROWN AWAY.

WHAT THE DOCTOR RECOMMENDED.

WANTED TO FEEL SAFE.

PREFERRED TO TRAMP ON FOOT.

and everybody rushed out to take charge of him, but he said, 'Never mind,' and jumped out and told the coachman to wait,—said he hadn't time to take anything to eat, he only had a little claim against the government to collect, would run across the way, to the Treasury, and fetch the money, and then get right along back to Tennessee, for he was in considerable of a hurry.

"Well, about eleven o'clock that night he came back and ordered a bed and told them to put the horses up,—said he would collect the claim in the morning. This was in January, you understand,—January, 1834,—the 3d of January,—Wednesday.

"Well, on the 5th of February, he sold the fine carriage, and bought a cheap second-hand one,—said it would answer just as well to take the money home in, and he didn't care for style.

"On the 11th of August he sold a pair of the fine horses,—said he'd often thought a pair was better than four, to go over the rough mountain roads with where a body had to be careful about his driving,—and there wasn't so much of his claim but he could lug the money home with a pair easy enough.

"On the 13th of December he sold another horse,—said two warn't necessary to drag that old light vehicle with,—in fact, one could snatch it along faster than was absolutely necessary, now that it was good solid winter weather and the roads in splendid condition.

"On the 17th of February, 1835, he sold the old carriage and bought a cheap second-hand buggy,—said a buggy was just the trick to skim along mushy, slushy early spring roads with, and he had always wanted to try a buggy on those mountain roads, anyway.

"On the 1st of August he sold the buggy and bought the remains of an old sulky,—said he just wanted to see those green Tennesseans stare and gawk when they saw him come a-ripping along in a sulky,—didn't believe they'd ever heard of a sulky in their lives.

"Well, on the 29th of August he sold his colored coachman,—said he didn't need a coachman for a sulky,—wouldn't be room enough for two in it anyway,—and, besides, it wasn't every day that Providence sent a man a fool who was willing to pay nine hundred dollars for such a third-rate negro as that,—been wanting to get rid of the creature for years, but didn't like to throw him away.

"Eighteen months later,—that is to say, on the 15th of February, 1837,—he sold the sulky and bought a saddle,—said horseback riding was what the doctor had always recommended him to take, and dog'd if he wanted to risk his neck going over those mountain roads on wheels in the dead of winter, not if he knew himself.

"On the 9th of April he sold the saddle,—said he wasn't going to risk his life with any perishable saddle-girth that ever was made, over a rainy, miry April road, while he could ride bareback and know and feel he was safe,—always had despised to ride on a saddle, anyway.

"On the 24th of April he sold his horse,—said 'I'm just 57 to-day, hale and hearty,—it would be a pretty howdy-do for me to be wasting such a trip as that and such weather as this, on a horse, when there ain't anything in the world so splendid as a tramp on foot through the fresh spring woods and over the cheery mountains, to a man that is a man,—and I can make my dog carry my claim in a little bundle, anyway, when it's collected. So to-morrow I'll be up bright and early, make my little old collection, and mosey off to Tennessee, on my own hind legs, with a rousing Good-bye to Gadsby's.'

"On the 22d of June he sold his dog,—said 'Dern a dog, anyway, where you're just starting off on a rattling bully pleasure-tramp through the summer woods and hills,—perfect nuisance,—chases the squirrels, barks at everything, goes a-capering and splattering around in the fords,—man can't get any chance to reflect and enjoy nature,—and I'd a blamed sight ruther carry the claim myself, it's a mighty sight safer; a dog's mighty uncertain in a financial way,—always noticed it,—well, good-bye, boys,—last call,—I'm off for Tennessee with a good leg and a gay heart, early in the morning!'"

—*A Tramp Abroad* (1880), chapter 26

After finishing his story, Riley reveals to the job seeker that the man in his story had expected to settle his claim and be off to Tennessee more than thirty years earlier, but he's still in Washington waiting to settle his claim. He advises the job seeker to put up at Gadsby's and be patient.

"His tail has been chopped off or else he has sat down on it too hard, some time or other, and he has to fight the flies with his heels."

PART IV

SORRY STEEDS

Mark Twain was an exceptionally observant writer. One of the qualities that makes his writing so interesting and fun to read is his knack—indeed, his genius—for noticing things that others are likely to overlook and then describing them in novel and unexpected ways. If his writings about horses tend to emphasize animals with odd defects or peculiar behaviors, we should rejoice, as those characteristics are what make Mark Twain fun to read. If all the horses he writes about were strong, healthy, disciplined, and reliable mounts, they would soon become boring. Well, tighten your saddle cinch because the sorry steeds in this section are anything but boring. As a group, they exhibit every kind of equine flaw imaginable, and we can be sure that Mark Twain doesn't overlook anything.

"Within the hour, we found that it would not only be better, but was absolutely necessary, that we four, taking turns, two at a time, should put our hands against the end of the wagon and push it through the sand, leaving the feeble horses little to do but keep out of the way and hold up the tongue."

15

PUTTING THE CART BEFORE THE HORSES

This passage about Mark Twain's first serious prospecting venture in Nevada describes what may have been his earliest serious efforts to drive harnessed horses. Unfortunately, that venture didn't last long, as the prospectors' worn-out collection of draft animals proved better suited for being pushed than for pulling.

Hurry, was the word! We wasted no time. Our party consisted of four persons—a blacksmith sixty years of age, two young lawyers, and myself. We bought a wagon and two miserable old horses. We put eighteen hundred pounds of provisions and mining tools in the wagon and drove out of Carson on a chilly December afternoon. The horses were so weak and old that we soon found that it would be better if one or two of us got out and walked. It was an improvement. Next, we found that it would be better if a third man got out. That was an improvement also. It was at this time that I volunteered to drive, although I had never driven a harnessed horse before and many a man in such a position would have felt fairly excused from such a responsibility. But in a little while it was found that it would be a fine thing if the driver got out and walked also. It was at this time that I resigned the position of driver, and never resumed it again. Within the hour, we found that it would not only be better, but was absolutely necessary, that we four, taking turns, two at a time, should put our hands against the end of the wagon and push it through the sand, leaving the feeble horses little to do but keep out of the way and hold up the tongue. Perhaps it is well for one to know his fate at first, and get reconciled to it. We had learned ours in one afternoon. It was plain that we had to walk through the sand and shove that wagon and those horses two hundred miles. So we accepted the situation, and from that time forth we never rode. More than that, we stood regular and nearly constant watches pushing up behind.

We made seven miles, and camped in the desert. Young Clagett (now member of Congress from Montana) unharnessed and fed and watered the horses; Oliphant and I cut sage-brush, built the fire and brought water to cook with; and old Mr. Ballou the blacksmith did the cooking. This division of labor, and this appointment, was adhered to throughout

The Humboldt prospecting team pausing for a rest.

the journey. We had no tent, and so we slept under our blankets in the open plain. We were so tired that we slept soundly.

We were fifteen days making the trip—two hundred miles; thirteen, rather, for we lay by a couple of days, in one place, to let the horses rest. We could really have accomplished the journey in ten days if we had towed the horses behind the wagon, but we did not think of that until it was too late, and so went on shoving the horses and the wagon too when we might have saved half the labor. Parties who met us, occasionally, advised us to put the horses in the wagon, but Mr. Ballou, through whose iron-clad earnestness no sarcasm could pierce, said that that would not do, because the provisions were exposed and would suffer, the horses being "bituminous from long deprivation." The reader will excuse me from translating. What Mr. Ballou customarily meant, when he used a long word, was a secret between himself and his Maker. He was one of the best and kindest hearted men that ever graced a humble sphere of life.

—*Roughing It* (1872), chapter 27

WORLD'S WORST ROADWAY

"They imposed another pirate upon us at Nazareth—another invincible Arab guard. We took our last look at the city, clinging like a whitewashed wasp's nest to the hill-side, and at eight o'clock in the morning, departed. We dismounted and drove the horses down a bridle-path which I think was fully as crooked as a corkscrew; which I know to be as steep as the downward sweep of a rainbow, and which I believe to be the worst piece of road in the geography, except one in the Sandwich Islands, which I remember painfully, and possibly one or two mountain trails in the Sierra Nevadas. Often, in this narrow path, the horse had to poise himself nicely on a rude stone step and then drop his fore-feet over the edge and down something more than half his own height. This brought his nose near the ground, while his tail pointed up toward the sky somewhere, and gave him the appearance of preparing to stand on his head. A horse can not look dignified in this position. We accomplished the long descent at last, and trotted across the great Plain of Esdraelon."

—*The Innocents Abroad* (1869), chapter 51

16

AN INFERNALLY LAZY BLOOD RELATION

This letter to his mother that Mark Twain wrote from Nevada in early 1862 tells about a horse so lazy he felt sure it was related to him. He may have been right in that surmise, as in addition to being lazy, the horse was evidently like him in also being a deep thinker.

Not because we were fond of it, ma—oh, no—but on Bunker's account. Bunker was the "near" horse on the larboard side. Named after the Attorney General of this Territory [Benjamin B. Bunker]. My horse—you are acquainted with him, by reputation, already—and I am sorry you do not know him personally, ma, for I feel towards him, sometimes, as if he were a blood relation of our family—he is so infernally lazy, you know—*my* horse—I was going to say, was the "off" horse on the starboard side. But it was on Bunker's account, principally, that we pushed behind the wagon. For whenever we came to a hard piece of road, that poor, lean, infatuated cuss would fall into a deep reverie about something or other, and stop perfectly still, and it would generally take a vast amount of black-snaking and shoving and profanity to get started again; and as soon as he was fairly underway, he would take up the thread of his reflections where he left off, and go on thinking, and pondering, and getting himself more and more mixed up

Mark Twain's last sight of the notoriously lazy Bunker.

and tangled in his subject, until he would get regularly stuck again, and stop to review the question.

And always in the meanest piece of road he could find.

In fact, Ma, that horse had something on his mind all the way to Humboldt; and he had not got rid of it when I left there—for when I departed, I saw him standing, solitary and alone, away up on the highest peak of a mountain, where no horse ever ventured before, with his pensive figure darkly defined against the sky—still thinking about it.

—letter to Jane Lampton Clemens, January 30, 1862

17

THE MONOTONY OF MULES

Mark Twain disliked all forms of monotony, including repetitious writing. Being only human, he does, of course, occasionally repeat himself, but a remarkable thing about his vast literary output is how infrequently he does that. Here he compares the monotony of writers overusing a famous literary cliche to that of troublesome animals in a Nevada mining camp. It may not be surprising that the chief offenders are mules.

So far, good. If any man has a right to feel proud of himself, and satisfied, surely it is I. For I have written about the Coliseum, and the gladiators, the martyrs, and the lions, and yet have never once used the phrase "butchered to make a Roman holyday." I am the only free white man of mature age, who has accomplished this since [Lord] Byron originated the expression.

Butchered to make a Roman holyday sounds well for the first seventeen or eighteen hundred thousand times one sees it in print, but after that it begins to grow tiresome. I find it in all the books concerning Rome—and here latterly it reminds me of Judge Oliver. Oliver was a young lawyer, fresh from the schools, who had gone out to the deserts of Nevada to begin life. He found that country, and our ways of life, there, in those early days, different from life in New England or Paris. But he put on a woollen shirt and strapped a navy revolver to his person, took to the bacon and beans of the country, and determined to do in Nevada as Nevada did. Oliver accepted the situation so completely that although he must have sorrowed over many of his trials, he never complained—that is, he never complained but once. He, two others, and myself, started to the new silver mines in the Humboldt mountains—he to be Probate Judge of Humboldt county, and we to mine. The distance was two hundred miles. It was dead of winter. We bought a two-horse wagon and put eighteen hundred pounds of bacon, flour, beans, blasting-powder, picks and shovels in it; we bought two sorry-looking Mexican "plugs," with the hair turned the wrong way and more corners on their bodies than there are on the mosque of Omar; we hitched up and started. It was a dreadful trip. But Oliver did not complain. The horses dragged the wagon two miles from town and then gave out. Then we three pushed the wagon seven miles, and Oliver moved ahead and pulled the horses after him by the bits. We complained, but Oliver did not. The ground was frozen, and it froze our backs while we slept; the wind swept across our faces and froze our noses. Oliver did not complain. Five days of pushing the wagon by day and freezing by night brought us to the bad part of the journey—the Forty Mile Desert, or the Great American Desert, if you please. Still, this mildest-mannered man that ever was, had not complained. We started across at eight in the morning, pushing through sand that had no bottom; toiling all day long by the wrecks of a thousand wagons, the skeletons of ten thousand oxen; by wagon-tires enough to hoop the Washington Monument to the top, and ox-chains enough to girdle Long Island; by human graves; with our throats parched always, with thirst; lips bleeding from the alkali dust; hungry, perspiring, and very, very weary—so weary that when we dropped in the sand every fifty yards to rest the horses, we could hardly keep from going to sleep—no complaints from Oliver: none the next morning at three o'clock, when we got across, tired to death. Awakened two or three nights afterward at midnight, in a narrow canon, by the snow falling on our faces, and appalled at the imminent danger of being "snowed in," we harnessed up and pushed on till eight in the morning, passed the "Divide" and knew we were saved. No complaints. Fifteen days of hardship and fatigue brought us to the end of the two hundred miles, and the Judge had not complained. We wondered if any thing could exasperate him. We built a Humboldt house. It is done in this way. You dig a square in the steep base of the mountain, and set up two

When the mule fell through the tent roof, the fire flew in every direction.

uprights and top them with two joists. Then you stretch a great sheet of "cotton domestic" from the point where the joists join the hill-side down over the joists to the ground; this makes the roof and the front of the mansion; the sides and back are the dirt walls your digging has left. A chimney is easily made by turning up one corner of the roof. Oliver was sitting alone in this dismal den, one night, by a sage-brush fire, writing poetry; he was very fond of digging poetry out of himself—or blasting it out when it came hard. He heard an animal's footsteps close to the roof; a stone or two and some dirt came through and fell by him. He grew uneasy and said "Hi!—clear out from there, can't you!"—from time to time. But by and by he fell asleep where he sat, and pretty soon a mule fell down the chimney! The fire flew in every direction, and Oliver went over backwards. About ten nights after that, he recovered confidence enough to go to writing poetry again. Again he dozed off to sleep, and again a mule fell down the chimney. This time, about half of that side of the house came in with the mule. Struggling to get up, the mule kicked the candle out and smashed most of the kitchen furniture, and raised considerable dust. These violent awakenings must have been annoying to Oliver, but he never complained. He moved to a mansion on the opposite side of the canon, because he had noticed the mules did not go there. One night about eight o'clock he was endeavoring to finish his poem, when a stone rolled in—then a hoof appeared below the canvas—then part of a cow—the after part. He leaned back in dread, and shouted "Hooy! hooy! get out of this!" and the cow struggled manfully—lost ground steadily—dirt and dust streamed down, and before Oliver could get well away, the entire cow crashed through on to the table and made a shapeless wreck of every thing!

Then, for the first time in his life, I think, Oliver complained. He said,

"This thing is growing monotonous!"

Then he resigned his judgeship and left Humboldt county. "Butchered to make a Roman holyday" has grown monotonous to me.

—*The Innocents Abroad* (1869), chapter 27

18

HORSE SENSE

After spending several years in California and Hawaii, Mark Twain returned to Nevada in 1866 on a lecture tour. Despite having recently learned a great deal more about horses in Hawaii, he, with a companion, again made the mistake of trusting their mounts to find their way home in the dark.

We visited the mining camps of Red Dog and You Bet, and returned to Nevada in the night, through a forest country cut up into innumerable roads. In our simplicity we depended on the horses to choose the route for themselves, because by many romantic books we had been taught a wild and absurd admiration for the instinct of that species of brute. The only instinct ours had was one which moved them to hunt for places where there wasn't any road, and it was unerring—it never failed them. However, our horses did not go lame. It was very singular. My experience of horses is that they never throw away a chance to go lame, and that in all respects they are well meaning and unreliable animals. I have also observed that if you refuse a high price for a favorite horse, he will go and lay down somewhere and die.

—letter to *San Francisco Bulletin*, December 6, 1866

The horse's only instinct was to look for places where there wasn't any road.

19

A MAGNIFICENT RUIN!

During Mark Twain's cross-country trek through the Holy Land with his Quaker City *companions in 1867, one of the first stops before passing through Damascus was at Baalbec, an ancient Lebanese city whose stone ruins impressed him so much that he devoted an entire chapter of* The Innocents Abroad *to the site. The rest of the journey might have been an unmitigated pleasure, were it not for the travelers' broken-down horses—on several of which Mark Twain bestowed memorable names, such as "Jericho" (whom we shall meet later).*

We left Damascus at noon and rode across the plain. . . .

But, honestly, I think an umbrella is a nuisance any where when its business is to keep the sun off. No Arab wears a brim to his fez, or uses an umbrella, or any thing to shade his eyes or his face, and he always looks comfortable and proper in the sun. But of all the ridiculous sights I ever have seen, our party of eight is the most so—they do cut such an outlandish figure. They travel single file; they all wear the endless white rag of Constantinople wrapped round and round their hats and dangling down their backs; they all wear thick green spectacles, with side-glasses to them; they all hold white umbrellas, lined with green, over their heads; without exception their stirrups are too short—they are the very worst gang of horsemen on earth; their animals to a horse trot fearfully hard—and when they get strung out one after the other; glaring straight ahead and breathless; bouncing high and out of turn, all along the line; knees well up and stiff, elbows flapping like a rooster's that is going to crow, and the long file of umbrellas popping convulsively up and down—when one sees this outrageous picture exposed to the light of day, he is amazed that the gods don't get out their thunderbolts and destroy them off the face of the earth! I do—I wonder at it. I wouldn't let any such caravan go through a country of mine.

And when the sun drops below the horizon and the boys close their umbrellas and put them under their arms, it is only a variation of the picture, not a modification of its absurdity. . . .

But this last new horse I have got is trying to break his neck over the tent-ropes, and I shall have to go out and anchor him. Jericho and I have parted company. The new horse is not much to boast of, I think. One of his hind legs bends the wrong way, and the other one is as straight and stiff as a tent-pole. Most of his teeth are gone, and he is as blind as a bat. His nose has been broken at some time or other, and is arched like a culvert now. His under lip hangs down like a camel's, and his ears are chopped off close to his head. I had some trouble at first to find a name for him, but I finally concluded to call him Baalbec, because he is such a magnificent ruin. I can not keep from talking about my horses, because I have a very long and tedious journey before me, and they naturally occupy my thoughts about as much as matters of apparently much greater importance.

Mark Twain's new horse was not much to boast of.

We satisfied our pilgrims by making those hard rides from Baalbec to Damascus, but Dan's horse and Jack's were so crippled we had to leave them behind and get fresh animals for them. The dragoman says Jack's horse died. I swapped horses with Mohammed, the kingly-looking Egyptian who is our Ferguson's lieutenant. By Ferguson I mean our dragoman Abraham, of course. I did not take this horse on account of his personal appearance, but because I have not seen his back. I do not wish to see it. I have seen the backs of all the other horses, and found most of them covered with dreadful saddleboils which I know have not been washed or doctored for years. The idea of riding all day long over such ghastly inquisitions of torture is sickening. My horse must be like the others, but I have at least the consolation of not knowing it to be so.

I hope that in future I may be spared any more sentimental praises of the Arab's idolatry of his horse. In boyhood I longed to be an Arab of the desert and have a beautiful mare, and call her Selim or Benjamin or Mohammed, and feed her with my own hands, and let her come into the tent, and teach her to caress me and look fondly upon me with her great tender eyes; and I wished that a stranger might come at such a time and offer me a hundred thousand dollars for her, so that I could do like the other Arabs—hesitate, yearn for the money, but overcome by my love for my mare, at last say, "Part with thee, my beautiful one! Never with my life! Away, tempter, I scorn thy gold!" and then bound into the saddle and speed over the desert like the wind!

But I recall those aspirations. If these Arabs be like the other Arabs, their love for their beautiful mares is a fraud. These of my acquaintance have no love for their horses, no sentiment of pity for them, and no knowledge of how to treat them or care for them. The Syrian saddle-blanket is a quilted mattr[e]ss two or three inches thick. It is never removed from the horse, day or night. It gets full of dirt and hair, and becomes soaked with sweat. It is bound to breed sores. These pirates never think of washing a horse's back. They do not shelter the horses in the tents, either; they must stay out and take the weather as it comes. Look at poor cropped and dilapidated "Baalbec," and weep for the sentiment that has been wasted upon the Selims of romance!

—*The Innocents Abroad* (1869), chapter 45

"That this combination—of preacher and gray mare—should breed calamity, seems strange, and at first glance unbelievable; but the fact is fortified by so much unassailable proof that to doubt is to dishonor reason" (Life on the Mississippi, *chapter 25)*.

20

AN OLD GRAY MARE

In 1882, Mark Twain returned to the Mississippi River to gather material for Life on the Mississippi. *While steamboating down the river on the* Gold Dust, *he recorded this story from "Uncle Mumford," a fictitious character whom he modeled on the boat's real second mate, Dad Dunham. Whether the incident related here actually happened is impossible to confirm, but it's true that steamboatmen hated sailing with gray mares, especially in the company of preachers.*

Thebes, at the head of the Grand Chain, and Commerce at the foot of it, were towns easily rememberable, as they had not undergone conspicuous alteration. Nor the Chain, either—in the nature of things; for it is a chain of sunken rocks admirably arranged to capture and kill steamboats on bad nights. A good many steamboat corpses lie buried there, out of sight; among the rest my first friend the "Paul Jones"; she knocked her bottom out, and went down like a pot, so the historian told me—Uncle Mumford. He said she had a gray mare aboard, and a preacher. To me, this sufficiently accounted for the disaster; as it did, of course, to Mumford, who added,—

"But there are many ignorant people who would scoff at such a matter, and call it superstition. But you will always notice that they are people who have never travelled with a gray mare and a preacher. I went down the river once in such company. We grounded at Bloody

Several men throw the preacher overboard while others paint the mare blue.

Island; we grounded at Hanging Dog; we grounded just below this same Commerce; we jolted Beaver Dam Rock; we hit one of the worst breaks in the 'Graveyard' behind Goose Island; we had a roustabout killed in a fight; we burnt a boiler; broke a shaft; collapsed a flue; and went into Cairo with nine feet of water in the hold—may have been more, may have been less. I remember it as if it were yesterday. The men lost their heads with terror. They painted the mare blue, in sight of town, and threw the preacher overboard, or we should not have arrived at all. The preacher was fished out and saved. He acknowledged, himself, that he had been to blame. I remember it all, as if it were yesterday."

That this combination—of preacher and gray mare—should breed calamity, seems strange, and at first glance unbelievable; but the fact is fortified by so much unassailable proof that to doubt is to dishonor reason. I myself remember a case where a captain was warned by numerous friends against taking a gray mare and a preacher with him, but persisted in his purpose in spite of all that could be said; and the same day,—it may have been the next, and some say it was, though I think it was the same day,—he got drunk and fell down the hatchway and was borne to his home a corpse. This is literally true.

—*Life on the Mississippi* (1883), chapter 25

"I can easily understand, now, why that horse always looks so dejected and in different to the things of this world. They feed him on old newspapers."

PART V

ECCENTRIC EQUINES

Lest one think that every horse Mark Twain wrote about was problematic in one way or another, it should be remembered that he also wrote about equines with special qualities, many of which he lavishly praised. Here, for example, we meet a racehorse as remarkable as Jim Smiley's celebrated frog and a horse with an appetite so insatiable that even cats high up in trees aren't safe from it. We also encounter donkeys and mules willing to eat anything and horses confronting drinking water for the first time. Other animals that captured Mark Twain's respect include Egyptian donkeys shaven and painted in outlandish decorative patterns, as well as his favorite racing animals—New Orleans mules. Granted that not all these remarkable animals were real, but the fact that Mark Twain had good things to say about them confirms his underlying respect and admiration for horses and their equine kin.

A HORSE NAMED "MARK TWAIN"

"In a Sandwich Island paper just received by mail, I learn that some gentlemen of taste and enterprise, and also of Keokuk, Iowa, have named a fast young colt for me. Verily, one does have to go away from home to learn news. The cannibal paper adds that the colt has already trotted his mile, of his own accord, in 2:17 1–2. He was probably going to dinner at the time. The idea of naming anything that is fast after me—except an anchor or something of that kind—is a perfect inspiration of humor. If this poor colt could see me trot around the course one, he would laugh some of his teeth out—he would indeed, if he had time to wait till I finished the trip. I have seen slower people than I am—and more deliberate people than I am—and even quieter, and more listless, and lazier people than I am. But they were dead."

—"Favors from Correspondents," December 1870

21

THE FIFTEEN-MINUTE NAG

This anecdote comes from the sketch that helped make Mark Twain famous—his immortal jumping-frog story. First published in 1865, it contains what may be the first significant passage about a horse that Mark Twain ever wrote. Most of the sketch is about Smiley's gifted frog, Dan'l Webster, but being an inveterate gambler, Smiley also owns other remarkable animals on which he wagers, including a fighting dog and the mare described here.

Jim Smiley . . . was the curiosest man about always betting on anything that turned up you ever see, if he could get anybody to bet on the other side; and if he couldn't he'd change side—any way that suited the other man would suit him—any way just so's he got a bet, *he* was satisfied. But still, he was lucky—uncommon lucky; he most always come out winner. He was always ready and laying for a chance; there couldn't be no solitry thing mentioned but that feller'd offer to bet on it—and take any side you please, as I was just telling you. If there was a horse-race, you'd find him flush or you find him busted at the end of it; if there was a dog-fight, he'd bet on it; if there was a cat-fight, he'd bet on it; if there was a chicken-fight, he'd bet on it; why, if there was two birds setting on a fence, he would bet you which one would fly first. . . . Why, it never made no difference to him—he'd bet on *anything*—the dangest feller. . . .

Smiley's horse never came to life until it reached the fag-end of a race.

Thish-yer Smiley had a mare—the boys called her the fifteen-minute nag, but that was only in fun, you know, because of course she was faster than that—and he used to win money on that horse, for all she was so slow and always had the asthma, or the distemper, or the consumption, or something of that kind. They used to give her two or three hundred yards' start, and then pass her under way; but always at the fag-end of the race she'd get excited and desperate-like, and come cavorting and spraddling up, and scattering her legs around limber, sometimes in the air, and sometimes out to one side amongst the fences, and kicking up m-o-r-e dust and raising m-o-r-e racket with her coughing and sneezing and blowing her nose—and always fetch up at the stand just about a neck ahead, as near as you could cipher it down.

—"Jim Smiley and His Jumping Frog" (1865)

22

FITZ SMYTHE'S HUNGRY HOSS

After relocating from Nevada to California in 1864, Mark Twain spent several months reporting for San Francisco's Morning Call *newspaper. He worked with another man named Albert S. Evans, whom he liked to call "Fitz Smythe" in sketches he wrote as a correspondent for Virginia City's* Territorial Enterprise. *In 1866, he wrote this colorful but possibly exaggerated description of Fitz Smythe's ravenous horse.*

Yesterday, as I was coming along through a back alley, I glanced over a fence, and there was Fitz Smythe's horse. I can easily understand, now, why that horse always looks so dejected and in different to the things of this world. They feed him on old newspapers. I had often seen Smythe carrying "dead loads" of old exchanges up town, but I never suspected that they were to be put to such a use as this. A boy came up while I stood there, and said, "That hoss belongs to Mr. Fitz Smythe, and the old man—that's my father, you know—the old man's going to kill him."

"Who, Fitz Smythe?"

"No, the hoss—because he et up a litter of pups that the old man wouldn't a taken forty dol—"

"Who, Fitz Smythe?"

"No, the hoss—and he eats fences and everything—took our gate off and carried it home and et up every dam splinter of it; you wait till he gets done with them old Altas and Bulletins he's a chawin' on now, and you'll see him branch out and tackle a-n-y-thing he can shet his mouth on. Why, he nipped a little boy, Sunday, which was going home from Sunday school; well, the boy got loose, you know, but that old hoss got his bible and some tracts, and them's as good a thing as he wants, being so used to papers, you see. You put anything to eat anywheres, and that old hoss'll shin out and get it—and he'll eat anything he can bite, and he don't care a dam. He'd climb a tree, he would, if you was to put anything up there for him—cats, for instance—he likes cats—he's et up every cat there was here in four blocks—he'll take more chances—why, he'll bust in anywheres for one of them fellers; I see him snake a old tom cat out of that there flower-pot over yonder, where she was a sunning

Fitz Smythe's horse would climb a tree if it had anything it liked to eat.

of herself, and take her down, and she a hanging on and a grabbling for a holt on some thing, and you could hear her yowl and kick up and tear around after she was inside of him. You see Mr. Fitz Smythe don't give him nothing to eat but them old newspapers and sometimes a basket of shavings, and so you know, he's got to prospect or starve, and a hoss ain't going to starve, it ain't likely, on account of not wanting to be rough on cats and sich things. Not that hoss, anyway, you bet you. Because he don't care a dam. You turn him loose once on this town, and don't you know he'd eat up m-o-r-e goods-boxes, and fences, and clothing-store things, and animals, and all them kind of valuables? Oh, you bet he would. Because that's his style, you know, and he don't care a dam. But you ought to see Mr. Fitz Smythe ride him around, prospecting for them items—you ought to see him with his soldier coat on, and his mustashers sticking out strong like a cat-fish's horns, and them long laigs of his'n standing out so, like them two prongs they prop up a step-ladder with, and a jolting down street at four mile a week—oh, what a guy!—sets up stiff like a close pin, you know, and thinks he looks like old General Macdowl. But the old man's a going to hornisswoggle that hoss on account of his goblin up them pups. Oh, you bet your life the old man's down on him. Yes, sir, coming!" and the entertaining boy departed to see what the "old man" was calling him for. But I am glad that I met the boy, and I am glad I saw the horse taking his literary breakfast, because I know now why the animal looks so discouraged when I see Fitz Smythe rambling down Montgomery street on him—he has altogether too rough a time getting a living to be cheerful and frivolous or anyways frisky.

—letter to *Territorial Enterprise*, January 16–18, 1866

EXPENSIVE TASTES

Being unable to ride the untamable Mexican plug Mark Twain bought in Nevada wasn't the only disadvantage of its ownership, as Mark Twain later recalled, after "the livery stable man brought in his bill for six weeks' keeping—stall-room for the horse, fifteen dollars; hay for the horse, two hundred and fifty! The Genuine Mexican Plug had eaten a ton of the article, and the man said he would have eaten a hundred if he had let him.

"I will remark here, in all seriousness, that the regular price of hay during that year and a part of the next was really two hundred and fifty dollars a ton. During a part of the previous year it had sold at five hundred a ton, in gold, and during the winter before that there was such scarcity of the article that in several instances small quantities had brought eight hundred dollars a ton in coin! The consequence might be guessed without my telling it: people turned their stock loose to starve . . ."

—*Roughing It* (1872), chapter 34

23

APPETITES THAT NOTHING WILL SATISFY

Fitz Smythe's horse wasn't the only voracious animal that Mark Twain wrote about. The passage here from Roughing It *mixes reminiscences about donkeys and mules he met in Nevada during the early 1860s with a nod to camels he encountered in the Middle East about six years later. (It is immediately followed by a much longer discussion of the strange things camels eat. However, as biologists have not yet seen fit to classify camels as equines, and as Mark Twain seems never to have ridden one, it would be inappropriate to include the rest of that passage here.)*

I do not remember where we first came across "sage-brush," but as I have been speaking of it I may as well describe it. This is easily done, for if the reader can imagine a gnarled and venerable live oak-tree reduced to a little shrub two feet high, with its rough bark, its foliage, its twisted boughs, all complete, he can picture the "sage-brush" exactly. . . .

Sage-brush is very fair fuel, but as a vegetable it is a distinguished failure. Nothing can abide the taste of it but the jackass and his illegitimate child the mule. But their testimony to its nutritiousness is worth nothing, for they will eat pine knots, or anthracite coal, or brass filings, or lead pipe, or old bottles, or anything that comes handy, and then go off looking as grateful as if they had had oysters for dinner. Mules and donkeys and camels have appetites that anything will relieve temporarily, but nothing satisfy.

—*Roughing It* (1872), chapter 3

Jackasses and mules will eat anything *that comes handy.*

24

YOU CAN LEAD A HORSE TO WATER, BUT . . .

This anecdote from Mark Twain's time in Hawaii describes a phenomenon so extraordinary one is inclined to suspect he was hoaxing his readers. He was, however, probably telling the truth. Some horses raised high up in the islands' lush mountains really did grow up without ever drinking liquid water!

In one locality, on our journey, we saw some horses that had been born and reared on top of the mountains, above the range of running water, and consequently they had never drank that fluid in their lives, but had been always accustomed to quenching their thirst by eating dew-laden or shower-wetted leaves. And now it was destructively funny to see them sniff suspiciously at a pail of water, and then put in their noses and try to take a bite out of the fluid, as if it were a solid. Finding it liquid, they would snatch away their heads and fall to trembling, snorting and showing other evidences of fright. When they became convinced at last that the water was friendly and harmless, they thrust in their noses up to their eyes, brought out a mouthful of the water, and proceeded to *chew* it complacently. We saw a man coax, kick and spur one of them five or ten minutes before he could make it cross a running stream. It spread its nostrils, distended its eyes and trembled all over, just as horses customarily do in the presence of a serpent—and for aught I know it thought the crawling stream was a serpent.

—*Roughing It* (1872), chapter 76

Horses that have never drunk liquid water before will try to take a bite out of it, as if it were a solid.

25

THE SHIEST HORSE IN THE WORLD

Mark Twain rode a succession of problematic horses on his overland trek through the Holy Land in 1867. This anecdote concerns his first mount, Jericho, a remarkable animal in many ways, including, apparently, the fact that he *is a mare!*

We are camped near Temnin-el-Foka—a name which the boys have simplified a good deal, for the sake of convenience in spelling. They call it Jacksonville. It sounds a little strangely, here in the Valley of Lebanon, but it has the merit of being easier to remember than the Arabic name. . . .

While I am speaking of animals, I will mention that I have a horse now by the name of "Jericho." He is a mare. I have seen remarkable horses before, but none so remarkable as this. I wanted a horse that could shy, and this one fills the bill. I had an idea that shying indicated spirit. If I was correct, I have got the most spirited horse on earth. He shies at every thing he comes across, with the utmost impartiality. He appears to have a mortal dread of telegraph poles, especially; and it is fortunate that these are on both sides of the road, because as it is now, I never fall off twice in succession on the same side. If I fell on the same side always, it would get to be monotonous after a while. This creature has scared at every thing he has seen to-day, except a haystack. He walked up to that with an intrepidity and a recklessness that were

Jericho struggling to kick flies off its head.

astonishing. And it would fill any one with admiration to see how he preserves his self-possession in the presence of a barley sack. This dare-devil bravery will be the death of this horse some day.

He is not particularly fast, but I think he will get me through the Holy Land. He has only one fault. His tail has been chopped off or else he has sat down on it too hard, some time or other, and he has to fight the flies with his heels. This is all very well, but when he tries to kick a fly off the top of his head with his hind foot, it is too much variety. He is going to get himself into trouble that way some day. He reaches around and bites my legs too. I do not care particularly about that, only I do not like to see a horse too sociable.

I think the owner of this prize had a wrong opinion about him. He had an idea that he was one of those fiery, untamed steeds, but he is not of that character. I know the Arab had this idea, because when he brought the horse out for inspection in Beirout, he kept jerking at the bridle and shouting in Arabic, "Ho! will you? Do you want to run away, you ferocious beast, and break your neck?" when all the time the horse was not doing any thing in the world, and only looked like he wanted to lean up against something and think. Whenever he is not shying at things, or reaching after a fly, he wants to do that yet. How it would surprise his owner to know this.

—*The Innocents Abroad* (1869), chapter 42

26

STYLISH ASSES

Mark Twain's visit to Egypt in 1867 provided one of his most pleasant riding experiences and introduced him to some elaborately decorated animals. In contrast to many passages he wrote about horses, this one about the donkeys tourists rode to the pyramids has mostly good things to say about the animals. As we later see, however, not all his experiences with donkeys were happy ones.

The donkeys were all good, all handsome, all strong and in good condition, all fast and all willing to prove it. They were the best we had found any where, and the most recherche. I do not know what recherche is, but that is what these donkeys were, anyhow* Some were of a soft mouse-color, and the others were white, black, and vari-colored. Some were close-shaven, all over, except that a tuft like a paint-brush was left on the end of the tail. Others were so shaven in fanciful landscape garden patterns, as to mark their bodies with curving lines, which were bounded on one side by hair and on the other by the close plush left by the shears. They had all been newly barbered, and were exceedingly stylish. Several of the white ones were barred like zebras with rainbow stripes of blue and red and yellow paint. These were indescribably gorgeous. Dan and Jack selected from this lot

* A word of French origin, *recherche* means excessively refined or pretentious, and its use in English is itself somewhat pretentious—much like the Egyptian donkeys Mark Twain describes.

because they brought back Italian reminiscences of the "old masters." The saddles were the high, stuffy, frog-shaped things we had known in Ephesus and Smyrna. The donkey-boys were lively young Egyptian rascals who could follow a donkey and keep him in a canter half a day without tiring. We had plenty of spectators when we mounted, for the hotel was full of English people bound overland to India and officers getting ready for the African campaign against the Abyssinian King Theodorus. We were not a very large party, but as we charged through the streets of the great metropolis, we made noise for five hundred, and displayed

Some of the Egyptian donkeys were indescribably gorgeous.

activity and created excitement in proportion. Nobody can steer a donkey, and some collided with camels, dervishes, effendis, asses, beggars and every thing else that offered to the donkeys a reasonable chance for a collision. When we turned into the broad avenue that leads out of the city toward Old Cairo, there was plenty of room. . . .

Arrived at Old Cairo, the camp-followers took up the donkeys and tumbled them bodily aboard a small boat with a lateen sail, and we followed and got under way. The deck was closely packed with donkeys and men; the two sailors had to climb over and under and through the wedged mass to work the sails, and the steersman had to crowd four or five donkeys out of the way when he wished to swing his tiller and put his helm hard-down. But what were their troubles to us? We had nothing to do; nothing to do but enjoy the trip; nothing to do but shove the donkeys off our corns and look at the charming scenery of the Nile. . . .

The Nile at this point is muddy, swift and turbid, and does not lack a great deal of being as wide as the Mississippi.

We scrambled up the steep bank at the shabby town of Ghizeh, mounted the donkeys again, and scampered away. For four or five miles the route lay along a high embankment which they say is to be the bed of a railway the Sultan means to build for no other reason than that when the Empress of the French comes to visit him she can go to the Pyramids in comfort. This is true Oriental hospitality. I am very glad it is our privilege to have donkeys instead of cars.

At the distance of a few miles the Pyramids rising above the palms, looked very clean-cut, very grand and imposing, and very soft and filmy, as well. They swam in a rich haze that took from them all suggestions of unfeeling stone, and made them seem only the airy nothings of a dream—structures which might blossom into tiers of vague arches, or ornate colonnades, may be, and change and change again, into all graceful forms of architecture, while we looked, and then melt deliciously away and blend with the tremulous atmosphere.

At the end of the levee we left the mules [i.e., donkeys] and went in a sail-boat across an arm of the Nile or an overflow, and landed where the sands of the Great Sahara left their embankment, as straight as a wall, along the verge of the alluvial plain of the river.

—*The Innocents Abroad* (1869), chapter 58

"We assisted . . . at a mule race, one day. I believe I enjoyed this contest more than any other mule there. I enjoyed it more than I remember having enjoyed any other animal race I ever saw."

27

RACING MULES

Despite absentmindedly calling Egyptian donkeys "mules" in his account of his 1867 visit to the great pyramids, Mark Twain well knew the difference between the two types of equines. He generally didn't say many favorable things about mules—which he once called the "illegitimate child" of the jackass—but after seeing mules race in New Orleans in 1882, he had nothing but praise for them. (Mules, incidentally, can run nearly as fast as horses, especially if they are bred for speed.)

We assisted—in the French sense—at a mule race, one day. I believe I enjoyed this contest more than any other mule there. I enjoyed it more than I remember having enjoyed any other animal race I ever saw. The grand stand was well filled with the beauty and the chivalry of New Orleans. That phrase is not original with me. It is the Southern reporter's. He has used it for two generations. He uses it twenty times a day, or twenty thousand times a day; or a million times a day—according to the exigencies. He is obliged to use it a million times a day, if he have occasion to speak of respectable men and women that often; for he has no other phrase for such service except that single one. He never tires of it; it always has a fine sound to him. There is a kind of swell mediaeval bulliness and tinsel about it that pleases his gaudy barbaric soul. If he had been in Palestine in the early times, we should have had no references to "much people" out of him. No, he would have said "the beauty and the chivalry of Galilee" assembled to hear the Sermon on the Mount. It is likely that the men and women of the South are sick enough of that phrase by this time, and would like a change, but there is no immediate prospect of their getting it. . . .

But let us return to the mule. Since I left him, I have rummaged around and found a full report of the race. In it I find confirmation of the theory which I broached just now—namely, that the trouble with the Southern reporter is Women: Women, supplemented by Walter Scott and his knights and beauty and chivalry, and so on. This is an excellent report, as long as the women stay out of it. . . .

There were thirteen mules in the first heat; all sorts of mules, they were; all sorts of complexions, gaits, dispositions, aspects. Some were handsome creatures, some were not; some were sleek, some hadn't had their fur brushed lately; some were innocently gay and frisky; some were full of malice and all unrighteousness; guessing from looks, some of them thought the matter on hand was war, some thought it was a lark, the rest took it for a religious occasion. And each mule acted according to his convictions. The result was an absence of harmony well compensated by a conspicuous presence of variety—variety of a picturesque and entertaining sort.

All the riders were young gentlemen in fashionable society. If the reader has been wondering why it is that the ladies of New Orleans attend so humble an orgy as a mule-race, the thing is explained now. It is a fashion-freak; all connected with it are people of fashion.

It is great fun, and cordially liked. The mule-race is one of the marked occasions of the year. It has brought some pretty fast mules to the front. One of these had to be ruled out, because he was so fast that he turned the thing into a one-mule contest, and robbed it of one of its best features—variety. But every now and then somebody disguises him with a new name and a new complexion, and rings him in again.

The riders dress in full jockey costumes of bright-colored silks, satins, and velvets.

The thirteen mules got away in a body, after a couple of false starts, and scampered off with prodigious spirit. As each mule and each rider had a distinct opinion of his own as to how the race ought to be run, and which side of the track was best in certain circumstances, and how often the track ought to be crossed, and when a collision ought to be accomplished, and when it ought to be avoided, these twenty-six conflicting opinions created a most fantastic and picturesque confusion, and the resulting spectacle was killingly comical.

Each of the mules acting to its own convictions.

Mile heat; time, 2:22. Eight of the thirteen mules distanced. I had a bet on a mule which would have won if the procession had been reversed. The second heat was good fun; and so was the "consolation race for beaten mules," which followed later; but the first heat was the best in that respect.

The combination of thirteen mules and thirteen riders produced twenty-six conflicting opinions about how the race should be run.

I think that much the most enjoyable of all races is a steamboat race; but, next to that, I prefer the gay and joyous mule-rush. Two red-hot steamboats raging along, neck-and-neck, straining every nerve—that is to say, every rivet in the boilers—quaking and shaking and groaning from stem to stern, spouting white steam from the pipes, pouring black smoke from the chimneys, raining down sparks, parting the river into long breaks of hissing foam—this is sport that makes a body's very liver curl with enjoyment. A horse-race is pretty tame and colorless in comparison. Still, a horse-race might be well enough, in its way, perhaps, if it were not for the tiresome false starts. But then, nobody is ever killed. At least, nobody was ever killed when I was at a horse-race. They have been crippled, it is true; but this is little to the purpose.

—*Life on the Mississippi* (1883), chapter 45

"Down to its smallest details the [Wild West] show is genuine. . . . The effects produced upon me by its spectacles were identical with those wrought upon me a long time ago by the same spectacles on the frontier."

PART VI

DAREDEVIL RIDERS

By now it should be clear that Mark Twain himself was no daredevil when it came to horses. However, it should also be clear that he greatly admired the daredevilry of others, such as the picturesquely wild riders whom he saw when he first arrived in Nevada. Indeed, watching those men fly through the streets of Carson City inspired him to buy a horse of his own. His unfortunate experience with the Mexican plug he bought quelled his enthusiasm for becoming a wild rider himself, but he would still have plenty to say about other daring riders. Among the devil-may-care riders we meet here are a foolish would-be buffalo hunter and an even more foolish donkey rider who almost enters the wrong building. Others include the famous pony riders of the Old West and a colorful circus performer. Mark Twain also looks back at his Mexican plug and even describes his own bit of derring-do on a precipitous Alpine donkey trail.

*We "joined a party who were just starting on a buffalo hunt. It was noble sport galloping over the plain in the dewy freshness of the morning, but our part of the hunt ended in disaster and disgrace, for a wounded buffalo bull chased the passenger Bemis . . ." (*Roughing It*, chapter 7).*

28

BEMIS'S BUFFALO ADVENTURE

One of Roughing It*'s many flights of fancy describes a dangerous buffalo hunt during a break in the narrator's cross-country stagecoach trip to Nevada. In escaping from an enraged bull buffalo, a foolhardy greenhorn named Bemis (possibly a cousin of the hapless Blucher, whom we soon meet again) distinguished himself with his remarkable horsemanship. (It's a shame he wasn't riding Fitz Smythe's skilled tree-climbing horse.)*

Next morning, just before dawn, when about five hundred and fifty miles from St. Joseph, our mud-wagon broke down. We were to be delayed five or six hours, and therefore we took horses, by invitation, and joined a party who were just starting on a buffalo hunt. It was noble sport galloping over the plain in the dewy freshness of the morning, but our part of the hunt ended in disaster and disgrace, for a wounded buffalo bull chased the passenger Bemis nearly two miles, and then he forsook his horse and took to a lone tree. He was very sullen about the matter for some twenty-four hours, but at last he began to soften little by little, and finally he said:

"Well, it was not funny, and there was no sense in those gawks making themselves so facetious over it. I tell you I was angry in earnest for awhile. I should have shot that long gangly lubber they called Hank, if I could have done it without crippling six or seven other people—but of course I couldn't, the old 'Allen's' [pistol] so confounded comprehensive.

I wish those loafers had been up in the tree; they wouldn't have wanted to laugh so. If I had had a horse worth a cent—but no, the minute he saw that buffalo bull wheel on him and give a bellow, he raised straight up in the air and stood on his heels. The saddle began to slip, and I took him round the neck and laid close to him, and began to pray. Then he came down and stood up on the other end awhile, and the bull actually stopped pawing sand and bellowing to contemplate the inhuman spectacle. Then the bull made a pass at him and uttered a bellow that sounded perfectly frightful, it was so close to me, and that seemed to literally prostrate my horse's reason, and make a raving distracted maniac of him, and I wish I may die if he didn't stand on his head for a quarter of a minute and shed tears. He was absolutely out of his mind—he was, as sure as truth itself, and he really didn't know what he was doing. Then the bull came charging at us, and my horse dropped down on all fours

An angry buffalo chased the hapless Bemis nearly two miles.

and took a fresh start—and then for the next ten minutes he would actually throw one hand-spring after another so fast that the bull began to get unsettled, too, and didn't know where to start in—and so he stood there sneezing, and shovelling dust over his back, and bellowing every now and then, and thinking he had got a fifteen-hundred dollar circus horse for breakfast, certain. Well, I was first out on his neck—the horse's, not the bull's—and then underneath, and next on his rump, and sometimes head up, and sometimes heels—but I tell you it seemed solemn and awful to be ripping and tearing and carrying on so in the presence of death, as you might say. Pretty soon the bull made a snatch for us and brought away some of my horse's tail (I suppose, but do not know, being pretty busy at the time), but something made him hungry for solitude and suggested to him to get up and hunt for it. And then you ought to have seen that spider-legged old skeleton go! and you ought to have seen the bull cut out after him, too—head down, tongue out, tail up, bellowing like everything, and actually mowing down the weeds, and tearing up the earth, and boosting up the sand like a whirlwind! By George, it was a hot race! I and the saddle were back on the rump, and I had the bridle in my teeth and holding on to the pommel with both hands. First we left the dogs behind; then we passed a jackass rabbit; then we overtook a coyote, and were gaining on an antelope when the rotten girth let go and threw me about thirty yards off to the left, and as the saddle went down over the horse's rump he gave it a lift with his heels that sent it more than four hundred yards up in the air, I wish I may die in a minute if he didn't. I fell at the foot of the only solitary tree there was in nine counties adjacent (as any creature could see with the naked eye), and the next second I had hold of the bark with four sets of nails and my teeth, and the next second after that I was astraddle of the main limb and blaspheming my luck in a way that made my breath smell of brimstone. I had the bull, now, if he did not think of one thing. But that one thing I dreaded. I dreaded it very seriously. There was a possibility that the bull might not think of it, but there were greater chances that he would. I made up my mind what I would do in case he did. It was a little over forty feet to the ground from where I sat. I cautiously unwound the lariat from the pommel of my saddle—"

"Your saddle? Did you take your saddle up in the tree with you?"

"Take it up in the tree with me? Why, how you talk. Of course I didn't. No man could do that. It fell in the tree when it came down."

"Oh—exactly."

"Certainly. I unwound the lariat, and fastened one end of it to the limb. It was the very best green raw-hide, and capable of sustaining tons. I made a slip-noose in the other end, and then hung it down to see the length. It reached down twenty-two feet—half way to the ground. I then loaded every barrel of the Allen with a double charge. I felt satisfied. I said to myself, if he never thinks of that one thing that I dread, all right—but if he does, all right anyhow—I am fixed for him. But don't you know that the very thing a man dreads is the thing that always happens? Indeed it is so. I watched the bull, now, with anxiety—anxiety which no one can conceive of who has not been in such a situation and

Bemis climbed a tree to escape the buffalo, but to his surprise, the animal followed him.

felt that at any moment death might come. Presently a thought came into the bull's eye. I knew it! said I—if my nerve fails now, I am lost. Sure enough, it was just as I had dreaded, he started in to climb the tree—"

"What, the bull?"

"Of course—who else?"

"But a bull can't climb a tree."

"He can't, can't he? Since you know so much about it, did you ever see a bull try?"

"No! I never dreamt of such a thing."

"Well, then, what is the use of your talking that way, then? Because you never saw a thing done, is that any reason why it can't be done?"

"Well, all right—go on. What did you do?"

"The bull started up, and got along well for about ten feet, then slipped and slid back. I breathed easier. He tried it again—got up a little higher—slipped again. But he came at it once more, and this time he was careful. He got gradually higher and higher, and my spirits went down more and more. Up he came—an inch at a time—with his eyes hot, and his tongue hanging out. Higher and higher—hitched his foot over the stump of a limb, and looked up, as much as to say, 'You are my meat, friend.' Up again—higher and higher, and getting more excited the closer he got. He was within ten feet of me! I took a long breath,—and then said I, 'It is now or never.' I had the coil of the lariat all ready; I paid it out slowly, till it hung right over his head; all of a sudden I let go of the slack, and the slip-noose fell fairly round his neck! Quicker than lightning I out with the Allen and let him have it in the face. It was an awful roar, and must have scared the bull out of his senses. When the smoke cleared away, there he was, dangling in the air, twenty foot from the ground, and going out of one convulsion into another faster than you could count! I didn't stop to count, anyhow—I shinned down the tree and shot for home."

"Bemis, is all that true, just as you have stated it?"

"I wish I may rot in my tracks and die the death of a dog if it isn't."

"Well, we can't refuse to believe it, and we don't. But if there were some proofs—"

"Proofs! Did I bring back my lariat?"

"No."

"Did I bring back my horse?"

"No."

"Did you ever see the bull again?"

"No."

"Well, then, what more do you want? I never saw anybody as particular as you are about a little thing like that."

I made up my mind that if this man was not a liar he only missed it by the skin of his teeth.

—*Roughing It* (1872), chapter 7

29

PONY RIDERS

Among the truest daredevil riders with whom Mark Twain crossed paths during his time in the Far West were the fearless young men who rode for the fabled pony express—the pony riders. "Crossed paths," in fact, accurately describes his encounters with them during his stagecoach ride across the plains in 1861. However, though he clearly admired them, there is no reason to think that he ever wished to join them.

In a little while all interest was taken up in stretching our necks and watching for the "pony-rider"—the fleet messenger who sped across the continent from St. Joe to Sacramento, carrying letters nineteen hundred miles in eight days! Think of that for perishable horse and human flesh and blood to do! The pony-rider was usually a little bit of a man, brimful of spirit and endurance. No matter what time of the day or night his watch came on, and no matter whether it was winter or summer, raining, snowing, hailing, or sleeting, or whether his "beat" was a level straight road or a crazy trail over mountain crags and precipices, or whether it led through peaceful regions or regions that swarmed with hostile Indians, he must be always ready to leap into the saddle and be off like the wind! There was no idling-time for a pony-rider on duty. He rode fifty miles without stopping, by daylight, moonlight, starlight, or through the blackness of darkness—just as it happened. He rode a splendid horse that was born for a racer and fed

Pony riders carried nothing not absolutely necessary—not even weapons for protection.

and lodged like a gentleman; kept him at his utmost speed for ten miles, and then, as he came crashing up to the station where stood two men holding fast a fresh, impatient steed, the transfer of rider and mail-bag was made in the twinkling of an eye, and away flew the eager pair and were out of sight before the spectator could get hardly the ghost of a look. Both rider and horse went "flying light." The rider's dress was thin, and fitted close; he wore a "round-about," and a skull-cap, and tucked his pantaloons into his boot-tops like a race-rider. He carried no arms—he carried nothing that was not absolutely necessary, for even the postage on his literary freight was worth five dollars a letter. He got but little frivolous correspondence to carry—his bag had business letters in it, mostly. His horse was stripped of all unnecessary weight, too. He wore a little wafer of a racing-saddle, and no visible blanket. He wore light shoes, or none at all. The little flat mail-pockets strapped under the rider's thighs would each hold about the bulk of a child's primer. They held many an important business chapter and newspaper letter, but these were written on paper as airy and thin as gold-leaf, nearly, and thus bulk and weight were economized. The stage-coach traveled about a hundred to a hundred and twenty-five miles a day (twenty-four hours), the pony-rider about two hundred and fifty. There were about eighty pony-riders in the saddle all the time, night and day, stretching in a long, scattering procession from Missouri to California, forty flying eastward, and forty toward the west, and among them making four hundred gallant horses earn a stirring livelihood and see a deal of scenery every single day in the year.

We had had a consuming desire, from the beginning, to see a pony-rider, but somehow or other all that passed us and all that met us managed to streak by in the night, and so we heard only a whiz and a hail, and the swift phantom of the desert was gone before we could get our heads out of the windows. But now we were expecting one along every moment, and would see him in broad daylight. Presently the driver exclaims:

"Here he comes!"

Every neck is stretched further, and every eye strained wider. Away across the endless dead level of the prairie a black speck appears against the sky, and it is plain that it moves. Well, I should think so! In a second or two it becomes a horse and rider, rising and falling, rising and falling—sweeping toward us nearer and nearer—growing more and more distinct, more and more sharply defined—nearer and still nearer, and the flutter of the hoofs comes faintly to the ear—another instant a whoop and a hurrah from our upper deck, a wave of the rider's hand, but no reply, and man and horse burst past our excited faces, and go winging away like a belated fragment of a storm!

So sudden is it all, and so like a flash of unreal fancy, that but for the flake of white foam left quivering and perishing on a mail-sack after the vision had flashed by and disappeared, we might have doubted whether we had seen any actual horse and man at all, maybe.

—*Roughing It* (1872), chapter 8

A PRICELESS BLESSING

"We left Damascus at noon and rode across the plain a couple of hours, and then the party stopped a while in the shade of some fig-trees to give me a chance to rest. It was the hottest day we had seen yet—the sun-flames shot down like the shafts of fire that stream out before a blow-pipe; the rays seemed to fall in a steady deluge on the head and pass downward like rain from a roof. . . . All the desert glared so fiercely that my eyes were swimming in tears all the time. The boys had white umbrellas heavily lined with dark green. They were a priceless blessing. I thanked fortune that I had one, too, notwithstanding it was packed up with the baggage and was ten miles ahead. It is madness to travel in Syria without an umbrella."

—*The Innocents Abroad* (1869), chapter 45

30

A "MULE THING" TO BE RESPECTED

During Mark Twain's visit to Switzerland in 1878, he found himself hiking down an Alpine mountain trail so steep and narrow that only a true daredevil would have tried to ride down it. In fact, in a letter he wrote to his wife, he said people were "not allowed to ride down it." He and his companion, Joseph Twichell (whom he calls Harris in A Tramp Abroad*) spent seven hours walking down the trail, but he has plenty to say about the mules that squeezed by him along the way.*

We began our descent, now, by the most remarkable road I have ever seen. It wound in corkscrew curves down the face of the colossal precipice,—a narrow way, with always the solid rock wall at one elbow, and perpendicular nothingness at the other. We met an everlasting procession of guides, porters, mules, litters, and tourists climbing up this steep and muddy path, and there was no room to spare when you had to pass a tolerably fat mule. I always took the inside, when I heard or saw the mule coming, and flattened myself against the wall. I preferred the inside, of course, but I should have had to take it anyhow, because the mule prefers the outside. A mule's preference—on a precipice—is a thing to be respected. Well, his choice is always the outside. His life is mostly devoted to carrying bulky paniers and packages which rest against his body,—therefore he is habituated to taking the outside edge of mountain paths, to keep his bundles from rubbing against rocks or banks on the other. When he goes into the passenger business he absurdly clings to his old habit, and keeps one leg of his passenger always dangling over the great deeps of the lower world while that passenger's heart is in the highlands, so to speak. More than once I saw a mule's hind foot cave over the outer edge and send earth and rubbish into the bottomless abyss; and I noticed that upon these occasions the rider, whether male or female, looked tolerably unwell.

There was one place where an 18-inch breadth of light masonry had been added to the verge of the path, and as there was a very sharp turn, here, a panel of fencing had been set up there at some ancient time, as a protection. This panel was old and gray and feeble, and the light masonry had been loosened by recent rains. A young American girl came along on

No room to spare.

a mule, and in making the turn the mule's hind foot caved all the loose masonry and one of the fence posts overboard; the mule gave a violent lurch inboard to save himself, and succeeded in the effort, but that girl turned as white as the snows of Mont Blanc for a moment.

The path here was simply a groove cut into the face of the precipice; there was a four-foot breadth of solid rock under the traveler, and a four-foot breadth of solid rock just above his head, like the roof of a narrow porch; he could look out from this gallery and see a sheer summitless and bottomless wall of rock before him, across a gorge or crack a biscuit's toss in width,—but he could not see the bottom of his own precipice unless he lay down and projected his nose over the edge. I did not do this, because I did not wish to soil my clothes.

Every few hundred yards, at particularly bad places, one came across a panel or so of plank fencing; but they were always old and weak, and they generally leaned out over the chasm and did not make any rash promises to hold up people who might need support. There was one of these panels which had only its upper board left; a pedestrianizing English youth came tearing down the path, was seized with an impulse to look over the precipice, and without an instant's thought he threw his weight upon that crazy board. It bent outward a foot! I never made a gasp before that came so near suffocating me. The English youth's face simply showed a lively surprise, but nothing more. He went swinging along valleywards again, as if he did not know he had just swindled a coroner by the closest kind of a shave.

The Alpine litter is sometimes like a cushioned box made fast between the middles of two long poles, and sometimes it is a chair with a back to it and a support for the feet. It is carried by relays of strong porters. The motion is easier than that of any other conveyance. We met a few men and a great many ladies in litters; it seemed to me that most of the ladies looked pale and nauseated; their general aspect gave me the idea that they were patiently enduring a horrible suffering. As a rule, they looked at their laps, and left the scenery to take care of itself.

But the most frightened creature I saw, was a led horse that overtook us. Poor fellow, he had been born and reared in the grassy levels of the Kandersteg valley and had never seen anything like this hideous place before. Every few steps he would stop short, glance wildly out from the dizzy height, and then spread his red nostrils wide and pant as violently as if he had been running a race; and all the while he quaked from head to heel as with a palsy. He was a handsome fellow, and he made a fine statuesque picture of terror, but it was pitiful to see him suffer so.

This dreadful path has had its tragedy. Baedeker, with his customary overterseness, begins and ends the tale thus:

> The descent on horseback should be avoided. In 1861 a Comtesse d'Herlincourt fell from her saddle over the precipice and was killed on the spot.

We looked over the precipice there, and saw the monument which commemorates the event. It stands in the bottom of the gorge, in a place which has been hollowed out of the rock to protect it from the torrent and the storms. Our old guide never spoke but when spoken to, and then limited himself to a syllable or two, but when we asked him about this tragedy he showed a strong interest in the matter. He said the Countess was very pretty, and very young,—hardly out of her girlhood, in fact. She was newly married, and was on her bridal tour. The young husband was riding a little in advance; one guide was leading the husband's horse, another was leading the bride's. The old man continued:

> The guide that was leading the husband's horse happened to glance back, and there was that poor young thing sitting up staring out over the precipice; and her face began to bend downward a little, and she put up her two hands slowly and met it,—so,—and put them flat against her eyes,—so,—and then she sunk out of the saddle, with a sharp shriek, and one caught only the flash of a dress, and it was all over.

Then after a pause:

> Ah, yes, that guide saw these things,—yes, he saw them all. He saw them all, just as I have told you.

After another pause:

> Ah, yes, he saw them all. My God, that was me. I was that guide!

This had been the one event of the old man's life; so one may be sure he had forgotten no detail connected with it. We listened to all he had to say about what was done and what happened and what was said after the sorrowful occurrence, and a painful story it was.

—*A Tramp Abroad* (1880), chapter 35

SAGACITY OF STREET-CAR HORSES

"To-night your uncle Larry Hutton [a family friend and guidebook author] told about the sagacity of the street-car horses. At certain places it is necessary for the off-horse to step to one side & place himself on a low platform—then his weight turns a switch. The horses all know about this, now, & don't have to be ordered. When they come to one of those places the off-horse always steps aside of his own accord & mounts the platform—when the switch turns he steps off & trots away on his journey. Coming back, the other horse does the same."

—letter to Jean Clemens, December 28, 1893

"And the population of that town of Carson City in the sandy desert, was a mixed one. It consisted of all sorts of people—clergymen and burglars, and highwaymen, lawyers and liars and everything which goes to make things lively and to make life a joy.

"Among them were a great many of the predecessors of the cowboys who rode the Mexican saddle and swung the lariat. I saw these men come flying through the town every day, sitting their horses so easily, and as comfortable as in a rocking chair. The spectacle was picturesque and exhilarating to me who knew nothing about horses, and I wished I could be a horseman myself. I wished I could try that great art some day, to fly through the town with incredible swiftness and disappear next minute in a cloud of dust. I got possessed with the passion and desire to become a horseman."

—speech in Hamilton, Bermuda, April 9, 1908

31

THE MEXICAN PLUG REMEMBERED

Mark Twain described his daring but less-than-joyous ride on a genuine Mexican plug in the memorable reminiscence included earlier in this book. He never forgot that bumpy experience and alluded to it in this letter he wrote to William F. Cody, better known as "Buffalo Bill," after seeing Cody's Wild West show several times in Connecticut. This letter is of special historical interest, as it reveals exactly how much time Mark Twain figured he had spent on his Mexican plug.

Dear Mr. Cody—I have now seen your Wild West show two days in succession, and have enjoyed it thoroughly. It brought vividly back the breezy, wild life of the great plains and the Rocky Mountains and stirred me like a war song. Down to its smallest details the show is genuine—cowboys, vaqueros, Indians, stage-coach, costumes and all; it is wholly free from sham and insincerity, and the effects produced upon me by its spectacles were identical with those wrought upon me a long time ago by the same spectacles on the frontier. Your pony expressman was as tremendous an interest to me yesterday as he was twenty-three years ago when he used to come whizzing by from over the desert with his war news, and your bucking horses were even painfully real to me, as I rode one of those outrages once for nearly a quarter of a minute. It is often said on the other side of the water that none of the exhibitions which we send to England are purely and distinctively American. If you will take the Wild West show over there you can remove that reproach.

Yours truly,
Mark Twain

—letter to William F. Cody, September 10, 1884;
published in *Hartford Courant*, July 16, 1885

Mark Twain's fifteen seconds in the saddle may not sound like much, but it's nearly twice as long as riders must stay mounted to qualify for scores in modern rodeo competitions. William Cody appreciated Mark Twain's letter, as he used it to promote his show. It may even have influenced his decision to take his show to England and Europe—which he did many times, the first time in 1887.

Watching the Wild West show's stunt riders reminded Mark Twain of the fifteen seconds he had spent on a bucking horse.

32

A REAL BULLY CIRCUS

It is perhaps appropriate that the most daring horseback rider in Mark Twain's writings appears in a fictional circus, where an acrobat does things on a horse dangerous enough to terrify Huck Finn. This passage, incidentally, reveals both Huck's empathy for other human beings and his naivete and unreliability as a narrator, as he absolutely fails to understand what he is describing.

I went to the circus, and loafed around the back side till the watchman went by, and then dived in under the tent. I had a twenty-dollar gold piece and some other money, but I reckoned I better save, because there ain't no telling how soon you are going to need it, away from home and amongst strangers, that way. You can't be too careful. I ain't opposed to spending money on circuses, when there ain't no other way, but there ain't no use in wasting it on them.

It was a real bully circus. It was the splendidest sight that ever was, when they all come riding two and two, a gentleman and lady, side by side, the men just in their drawers and under-shirts, and no shoes nor stirrups, and resting their hands on their thighs, easy and comfortable—there must a' been twenty of them—and every lady with a lovely complexion, and perfectly beautiful, and looking just like a gang of real sure-enough queens, and dressed in clothes that cost millions of dollars, and just littered with diamonds. It was a powerful fine sight; I never see anything so lovely. And then one by one they got up and stood, and went a-weaving around the ring so gentle and wavy and graceful, the men looking ever so tall and airy and straight, and their heads bobbing and skimming along, away up there under the tentroof, and every lady's rose-leafy dress flapping soft and silky around her hips, and she looking like the most loveliest parasol.

And then faster and faster they went, all of them dancing, first one foot stuck out in the air and then the other, the horses leaning more and more, and the ring-master going round and round the centre-pole, cracking his whip and shouting "hi!—hi!" and the clown cracking jokes behind him; and by-and-by all hands dropped the reins, and every lady put her knuckles on her hips and every gentleman folded his arms, and then how the horses did lean over and hump themselves! And so, one after the other they all skipped off into the ring, and made the sweetest bow I ever see, and then scampered out, and everybody clapped their hands and went just about wild.

Well, all through the circus they done the most astonishing things; and all the time that clown carried on so it most killed the people. The ring-master couldn't ever say a word to him but he was back at him quick as a wink with the funniest things a body ever said; and how he ever could think of so many of them, and so sudden and so pat, was what I couldn't noway understand. Why, I couldn't a thought of them in a year. And by-and-by a drunk man tried to get into the ring—said he wanted to ride; said he could ride as well as anybody that ever was. They argued and tried to keep him out, but he wouldn't listen, and the whole show come to a standstill. Then the people begun to holler at him and make fun of him, and that made him mad, and he begun to rip and tear; so that stirred up the people, and a lot of men begun to pile down off of the benches and swarm towards the ring, saying, "Knock him down! throw him out!" and one or two women begun to scream. So, then, the ring-master he made a little speech, and said he hoped there wouldn't be no disturbance, and if the man would promise he wouldn't make no more trouble, he would let him ride, if he thought he could stay on the horse. So everybody laughed and said all right, and the man got on. The minute he was on, the horse begun to rip and tear and jump and cavort around, with two circus men hanging onto his bridle trying to hold him, and the drunk man hanging onto his neck, and his heels flying in the air every jump, and the whole crowd of people standing up shouting and laughing till the tears rolled down. And at last sure enough, all the circus men could do, the horse broke loose, and away he went like the very nation, round and round the ring, with that sot laying down on him and hanging to his neck with first one leg hanging most to the ground on one side, and then t'other one on t'other side, and the people just crazy. It warn't funny to me, though; I was all of a tremble to see his danger. But pretty soon he struggled up astraddle and grabbed the bridle, a-reeling this way and that; and the next minute he sprung up and dropped the bridle and stood! and the horse agoing like a house afire too. He just stood up there, a-sailing around as easy and comfortable as if he warn't ever drunk in his life—and then he begun to pull off his clothes and sling them. He shed them so thick they kind of clogged up the air, and altogether he shed seventeen suits. And then, there he was, slim and handsome, and dressed the gaudiest and prettiest you ever saw, and he lit into that horse with his whip and made him fairly hum—and finally skipped off, and made his bow and danced off to the dressing-room, and everybody just a-howling with pleasure and astonishment.

Then the ring-master he see how he had been fooled, and he was the sickest ring-master you ever see, I reckon. Why, it was one of his own men! He had got up that joke all out of his own head, and never let on to nobody. Well, I felt sheepish enough, to be took in so, but I wouldn't a been in that ringmaster's place, not for a thousand dollars. I don't know; there may be bullier circuses than what that one was, but I never struck them yet. Anyways it was plenty good enough for me; and wherever I run across it, it can have all of my custom, every time.

—*Huckleberry Finn* (1884), chapter 22

The moment the drunk man climbed on the horse, the animal began to rip and tear.

One of Mark Twain's most outstanding horsemanship traits may have been getting lost.

PART VII

UNHAPPY HORSEY HAPPENSTANCES

Mark Twain once called *accident* a "word which I constantly make use of when I am talking to myself about the chain of incidents which has constituted my life." That word certainly applies to many of the equine misadventures he describes in his writings. He himself never had a really serious accident with a horse, but both of his horse-loving daughters did. Clara was twice thrown from horse-drawn conveyances—from a Hansom cab in London and from a sleigh in Connecticut. Her sister Jean was so seriously injured when her horse was killed running into a trolley car in 1904 that she apparently never rode a horse again. Happily, the stories in this section concern less disturbing mishaps involving both Mark Twain and other riders. Here readers will learn how horses can be smarter than humans in finding their way around, what makes nighttime riding more dangerous than daytime riding, and why riding horses and donkeys in the Dead Sea or near places of worship is a bad idea.

THE FAMILY'S WOULD-BE JOCKEY

Mark Twain's youngest daughter, Jean, was his family's most devoted animal lover and horse person. When she was ten years old, he wrote in a letter to a family friend, "We haven't forecast Jean's future yet, but think she is going to be a horse jockey & live in the stable." Jean never lived an a stable or became a jockey, but she remained an enthusiastic equestrian until 1904, when a near-fatal riding accident ended her riding career after her horse—apparently dazzled by its lights—ran into a streetcar in Lee, Massachusetts.

33

LOST IN THE DARK

A few months after his arrival in Nevada in mid-1861, Mark Twain wrote this letter to his sister to report his progress in silver prospecting. The venture it describes was apparently one of the first of many times when a horse let him down. He also didn't think much of one of his companions on that occasion—Attorney General Bunker—whom he later called the "densest intellect the President ever conferred upon the Territory." He even dubbed the horse he called his "infernally lazy blood relation" Bunker.

What we want now is something [a mining claim] that will commence paying immediately. We have got a chance to get into a claim where they say a tunnel has been run 150 feet, and the ledge struck. I got a horse yesterday, and went out with the Attorney-General [Benjamin B. Bunker] and the claim-owner [Clement T. Rice]—and we tried to go to the claim by a new route, and got lost in the mountains—sunset overtook us before we found the claim—my horse got too lame to carry me, and I got down and drove him ahead of me till within four miles of town—then we sent Rice on ahead. Bunker (whose horse was in good condition) undertook to lead mine, and I followed after him. Darkness shut him out from my view in less than a minute, and within the next minute I lost the road and got to wandering in the sage brush. I would find the road occasionally and then lose it again in a minute or so. I got to Carson about nine o'clock, at night, but

Wandering in the sagebrush.

not by the road I traveled when I left it. The General says my horse did very well for awhile, but soon refused to lead. Then he dismounted, and had a jolly time driving both horses ahead of him and chasing them here and there through the sage brush (it does my soul good when I think of it) until he got to town, when both animals deserted him, and he cursed them handsomely and came home alone. Of course the horses went to their stables.

—letter to Pamela Moffett, October 25, 1861

34

THE HORSES KNOW THE WAY . . .

One of Mark Twain's most outstanding horsemanship talents during his time in the Far West seems to have been getting lost. Here he describes a frightening mishap that occurred when he and two fellow silver prospectors got caught in a blizzard in Nevada. The incident answers the question of who has the better sense of direction—a man or a horse? (Hint: Horse lovers should love the answer.)

We seemed to be in a road, but that was no proof. We tested this by walking off in various directions—the regular snow-mounds and the regular avenues between them convinced each man that *he* had found the true road, and that the others had found only false ones. Plainly the situation was desperate. We were cold and stiff and the horses were tired. We decided to build a sage-brush fire and camp out till morning. This was wise, because if we were wandering from the right road and the snow-storm continued another day our case would be the next thing to hopeless if we kept on.

All agreed that a camp fire was what would come nearest to saving us, now, and so we set about building it. We could find no matches, and so we tried to make shift with the pistols. Not a man in the party had ever tried to do such a thing before, but not a man in the party doubted that it *could* be done, and without any trouble—because every man in the party had read about it in books many a time and had naturally come

The prospectors losing their way in the blizzard.

to believe it, with trusting simplicity, just as he had long ago accepted and believed *that other* common book-fraud about Indians and lost hunters making a fire by rubbing two dry sticks together.

We huddled together on our knees in the deep snow, and the horses put their noses together and bowed their patient heads over us; and while the feathery flakes eddied down and turned us into a group of white statuary, we proceeded with the momentous experiment. We broke twigs from a sage bush and piled them on a little cleared place in the shelter of our bodies. In the course of ten or fifteen minutes all was ready, and then, while conversation ceased and our pulses beat low with anxious suspense, Ollendorff applied his revolver, pulled the trigger and blew the pile clear out of the county! It was the flattest failure that ever was.

This was distressing, but it paled before a greater horror—the horses were gone! I had been appointed to hold the bridles, but in my absorbing anxiety over the pistol experiment I had unconsciously dropped them and the released animals had walked off in the storm. It was useless to try to follow them, for their footfalls could make no sound, and one could pass within two yards of the creatures and never see them. We gave them up without an effort at recovering them, and cursed the lying books that said horses would stay by their masters for protection and companionship in a distressful time like ours. . . .

After more failed attempts to start a fire, the prospectors resigned themselves to death and pledged mutually to forgive one another for past wrongs and to renounce their individual vices. Ollendorff threw away his whisky bottle, the inveterate card player Ballou threw away his pack of cards, and Mark Twain himself swore off smoking and threw away his pipe. Then . . .

We put our arms about each other's necks and awaited the warning drowsiness that precedes death by freezing.

It came stealing over us presently, and then we bade each other a last farewell. A delicious dreaminess wrought its web about my yielding senses, while the snow-flakes wove a winding sheet about my conquered body. Oblivion came. The battle of life was done.

I do not know how long I was in a state of forgetfulness, but it seemed an age. A vague consciousness grew upon me by degrees, and then came a gathering anguish of pain in my limbs and through all my body. I shuddered. The thought flitted through my brain, "this is death—this is the here-after."

Then came a white upheaval at my side, and a voice said, with bitterness:

"Will some gentleman be so good as to kick me behind?"

The saddled and bridled horses stood not fifteen steps away!

It was Ballou—at least it was a towzled snow image in a sitting posture, with Ballou's voice.

I rose up, and there in the gray dawn, not fifteen steps from us, were the frame buildings of a stage station, and under a shed stood our still saddled and bridled horses!

An arched snow-drift broke up, now, and Ollendorff emerged from it, and the three of us sat and stared at the houses without speaking a word. We really had nothing to say. We were like the profane man who could not "do the subject justice," the whole situation was so painfully ridiculous and humiliating that words were tame and we did not know where to commence anyhow.

The joy in our hearts at our deliverance was poisoned; well-nigh dissipated, indeed. We presently began to grow pettish by degrees, and sullen; and then, angry at each other, angry at ourselves, angry at everything in general, we moodily dusted the snow from our clothing and in unsociable single file plowed our way to the horses, unsaddled them, and sought shelter in the station.

I have scarcely exaggerated a detail of this curious and absurd adventure. It occurred almost exactly as I have stated it. We actually went into camp in a snow-drift in a desert, at midnight in a storm, forlorn and hopeless, within fifteen steps of a comfortable inn.

For two hours we sat apart in the station and ruminated in disgust. The mystery was gone, now, and it was plain enough why the horses had deserted us. Without a doubt they were under that shed a quarter of a minute after they had left us, and they must have overheard and enjoyed all our confessions and lamentations.

—*Roughing It* (1872), chapters 32–33

After breakfasting and recovering their strength, all three men quickly reverted to their old vices and agreed "to say no more about 'reform.'"

35

A WELL-BRED HORSE VS. AN UNDERBRED RIDER

One of Mark Twain's closest friends in Nevada was William Wright, a fellow Territorial Enterprise reporter who used the pen name Dan De Quille. The two reporters occasionally engaged in a mock rivalry. In April 1864, shortly before Mark Twain relocated to San Francisco, he tried to embarrass Wright by making fun of the latter's accident on a horse. This account comes from biographer Albert Bigelow Paine's discussion of the playful rivalries among Virginia City reporters.

Reference has already been made to the fashion among Virginia City papers of permitting reporters to use the editorial columns for ridicule of one another. This custom was especially in vogue during the period when Dan De Quille and Mark Twain and The Unreliable [*Union* reporter Clement T. Rice] were the shining journalistic lights of the Comstock. Scarcely a week went by that some apparently venomous squib or fling or long burlesque assault did not appear either in the *Union* or the *Enterprise*, with one of those jokers as its author and another as its target. . . .

These were the things that enlivened Comstock journalism. Once in a boxing bout Mark Twain got a blow on the nose which caused it to swell to an unusual size and shape. He went out of town for a few days, during which De Quille published an extravagant account of his

Even the cats and the chickens laughed when they saw De Quille ride by.

misfortune, describing the nose and dwelling on the absurdity of Mark Twain's ever supposing himself to be a boxer.

De Quille scored heavily with this item, but his own doom was written. Soon afterward he was out riding and was thrown from his horse and bruised considerably. This was Mark's opportunity. He gave an account of Dan's disaster; then commenting, he said:

> The idea of a plebeian like Dan supposing he could ever ride a horse! He! why, even the cats and the chickens laughed when they saw him go by. Of course, he would be thrown off. Of course, any well-bred horse wouldn't let a common, under-bred person like Dan stay on his back! When they gathered him up he was just a bag of scraps, but they put him together, and you'll find him at his old place in the *Enterprise* office next week, still laboring under the delusion that he's a newspaper man.

—Albert Bigelow Paine, *Mark Twain: A Biography* (1912), chapter 42; quote from Mark Twain's "Dan Reassembled," *Territorial Enterprise*, April 30, 1864

36

A HORSE OF THE "SPANISH PERSUASION"

Not long after settling in San Francisco, Mark Twain found himself being overworked as a beat reporter for the city's Morning Call *newspaper, which didn't allow him the creative freedom he had enjoyed while reporting for the* Territorial Enterprise. *Nevertheless, a careful read of this otherwise routine account of a horse-and-cart accident reveals both his irrepressible wit and his contempt for the cart's careless and cruel driver.*

Yesterday morning, a horse and cart were carelessly left unhitched and unwatched in Dupont street. The horse, being of the Spanish persuasion and not to be depended on, finally got tired standing idle, and ran away. He ran into Berry street, ran half a square and upset the cart, and fell, helplessly entangled in the harness. The vehicle was somewhat damaged, but two or three new wheels, some fresh sides, and a new bottom, will make it all right again. Considering the fact that little short narrow Berry street contains as many small children as all the balance of San Francisco put together, it is strange the frantic horse did not hash up a dozen or two of them in his reckless career. They all escaped, however, by the singular accident of being out of the way at the time, and they visited the wreck in countless swarms, after the disaster, and examined it with unspeakable satisfaction. The driver is a man of extraordinary intellect and mature judgment—he

Children visited the wreck in swarms and examined it with unspeakable satisfaction.

set his cart on its legs again as well as he could, and then whipped his horse until it was easy to see that the poor brute began to comprehend that something was up, though it is questionable whether he has yet cyphered out what that something was, or not. The driver, as we said before, was not in his wagon at the time of the accident, which accounts for the misfortune of his not being hurt in the least.

—"Runaway," *San Francisco Daily Morning Call*, July 14, 1864

"My uncle William (now deceased, alas!) used to say that a good horse was a good horse until it had run away once, and that a good watch was a good watch until the repairers got a chance at it. And he used to wonder what became of all the unsuccessful tinkers, and gunsmiths, and shoemakers, and engineers, and blacksmiths; but nobody could ever tell him."

—"My Watch" (1870)

37

A BIG VICIOUS COLT

Experienced horse people should appreciate this account of the perils of adjusting a saddle and mounting it in the dark. As Mark Twain demonstrates here, those perils are magnified in the pitch darkness of a moonless tropical night—especially when the horse is spirited and the rider is as inexperienced with horses as he was on the island of Maui in 1866.

My Dear Mother & Sister:

11 o'clock at Night.—This is the infernalest darkest country, when the moon don't shine; I stumbled & fell over my horse's lariat a minute ago & hurt my leg, so I must stay here tonight; I went to Ulapalakua Plantation (25 miles,) a few days ago, & returned yesterday afternoon to Mrs. Cornwell's (Waikapu Plantation) & staid all night . . . & came here this evening to Mrs. Peck's . . . & took tea, & we have been playing seven-up & whist . . . but I only hitched that horse, intending to ride to the further sea-shore . . . & stay all night at the Waihee Plantation . . . but as I said, I couldn't even see the horse it was so dark when I came out of Mr. Peck's a while ago, & so I fell & hurt my leg. I got the same leg hurt last week; I said I hadn't got hold of a spirited horse since I had been on the island, & one of the proprietors loaned me a big, vicious colt; he was altogether too spirited; I went to tighten the cinch before mounting him, when he let out with his left [leg] & kicked me across a ten-acre lot. A native rubbed & doctored me so well that I

was able to stand on my feet in half an hour. It was then half after 4, & I had an appointment to go 7 miles & get a girl & take her to a card party at 5. If I hadn't had a considerable weakness for her she might have gone to the devil under the circumstances, but as it was, I went after her. I got even with the colt; it was a very rough road, but I got there at 5 minutes past 5, & then had to quit, my leg hurt me so. She was ready & her horse was saddled, but we didn't go, but I had a jolly time—played cribbage nearly all night. If I were worth even $5,000 I would try to marry that plantation—but as it is, I resign myself to a long & useful bachlerdom as cheerfully as I may.

—letter to Jane Lampton Clemens and Pamela A. Moffett,
May 4, 1866

Mark Twain cinching the colt's saddle.

38

THE WORST PLACE TO RIDE A DONKEY

We first met Blucher when he was struggling to ride a donkey in the Azores. When the Quaker City *reached the Moroccan city of Tangier a week later, Blucher hadn't had enough time to master the art of donkey riding. On this occasion, his ineptitude nearly resulted in a real disaster.*

About the first adventure we had yesterday afternoon, after landing here, came near finishing that heedless Blucher. We had just mounted some mules and asses, and started out under the guardianship of the stately, the princely, the magnificent Hadji Mohammed Lamarty, (may his tribe increase!) when we came upon a fine Moorish mosque, with tall tower, rich with checker-work of many-colored porcelain, and every part and portion of the edifice adorned with the quaint architecture of the Alhambra, and Blucher started to ride into the open door-way. A startling "Hi-hi!" from our camp-followers, and a loud "Halt!" from an English gentleman in the party checked the adventurer, and then we were informed that so dire a profanation is it for a Christian dog to set foot upon the sacred threshold of a Moorish mosque, that no amount of purification can ever make it fit for the faithful to pray in again. Had Blucher succeeded in entering the place, he would no doubt have been chased through the town and stoned; and the time has been, and not many years ago either, when a

What might have happened if Mark Twain hadn't stopped Blucher from riding into the mosque!

Christian would have been most ruthlessly slaughtered, if captured in a mosque. We caught a glimpse of the handsome tessellated pavements within, and of the devotees performing their ablutions at the fountains; but even that we took that glimpse was a thing not relished by the Moorish bystanders.

—*The Innocents Abroad* (1869), chapter 9

The Quaker City *passenger whom Mark Twain calls Blucher in this passage was a sixty-seven-year-old Irish American named James G. Barry, who used the apparently honorary title of "major." In an 1868 letter to his mother and sister, Mark Twain wrote that he had been a "sort of benefactor to [Barry], once. I helped to snatch him out when he was about to ride into a Mohammedan Mosque in that queer old Moorish town of Tangier, in Africa. If he had got in, the Moors would have knocked his venerable old head off, for his temerity."*

39

TOPSY-TURVY HORSES

Anyone who has ever swum in a strongly saline body of water, such as Utah's Great Salt Lake, knows that everything one thinks one understands about buoyancy must be revised. That is even more true for horses, as Mark Twain explains in this description of swimming in the Holy Land's Dead Sea.

The Dead Sea is small. Its waters are very clear, and it has a pebbly bottom and is shallow for some distance out from the shores. It yields quantities of asphaltum; fragments of it lie all about its banks; this stuff gives the place something of an unpleasant smell.

All our reading had taught us to expect that the first plunge into the Dead Sea would be attended with distressing results—our bodies would feel as if they were suddenly pierced by millions of red-hot needles; the dreadful smarting would continue for hours; we might even look to be blistered from head to foot, and suffer miserably for many days. We were disappointed. . . .

No, the water did not blister us; it did not cover us with a slimy ooze and confer upon us an atrocious fragrance; it was not very slimy; and I could not discover that we smelt really any worse than we have always smelt since we have been in Palestine. . . .

It was a funny bath. We could not sink. One could stretch himself at full length on his back, with his arms on his breast, and all of his body above a line drawn from the corner of his jaw past the middle of his

Too top-heavy to stand upright in the Dead Sea, horses topple over instantly.

side, the middle of his leg and through his ankle bone, would remain out of water. He could lift his head clear out, if he chose. No position can be retained long; you lose your balance and whirl over, first on your back and then on your face, and so on. You can lie comfortably, on your back, with your head out, and your legs out from your knees down, by steadying yourself with your hands. You can sit, with your knees drawn up to your chin and your arms clasped around them, but you are bound to turn over presently, because you are top-heavy in that position. You can stand up straight in water that is over your head, and from the middle of your breast upward you will not be wet. But you can not remain so. The water will soon float your feet to the surface. You can not swim on your back and make any progress of any consequence, because your feet stick away above the surface, and there is nothing to propel yourself with but your heels. If you swim on your face, you kick up the water like a stern-wheel boat. You make no headway. A horse is so top-heavy that he can neither swim nor stand up in the Dead Sea. He turns over on his side at once.

—*The Innocents Abroad* (1869), chapter 55

"Out from his tent rode great Sir Sagramor, an imposing tower of iron."

PART VIII

WAR HORSES

The closest Mark Twain ever came to going to war himself occurred at the onset of the Civil War, when he was briefly a member of an informal militia troop. As we saw earlier, that was probably when he first learned horsemanship. Otherwise, his vast literary output contains comparatively little about war. His occasional remarks about war horses and their kin are both desultory and scattered, but he did manage to write about a number of horses that were at least trained for fighting. This section includes several fictional passages about medieval European war horses, including Joan of Arc's first mount and the steeds of King Arthur's knights, plus the personal narrative of a veteran US cavalry horse and Mark Twain's description of his own experience in a quasi-military situation in the Middle East. Finally, in his salute to Spanish-American War veterans, Mark Twain reveals what kind of steed he would want to ride if he were a "Rough Rider."

Mark Twain's Connecticut Yankee taking on the Tower of Iron.

40

SAINT JOAN LEARNS TO RIDE

Mark Twain's most extensive writing about war can be found in his 1896 novel about Joan of Arc, the legendary fourteenth-century peasant girl whom the French made a patron saint for her contributions to their eventual defeat of the English during the Hundred Years' War. Narrated by one of her devoted followers, the first passage here honors her memory by commenting on how rapidly she—in contrast to Mark Twain himself—mastered horsemanship. The second passage points out that not all the French peasants who followed her relished riding. It is easy to imagine Mark Twain identifying with the peasants. In fact, it is easy to imagine him recalling some of his own painful riding experiences as he described their suffering.

Already the people of Vaucouleurs had given her a horse and had armed and equipped her as a soldier. She got no chance to try the horse and see if she could ride it, for her great first duty was to abide at her post and lift up the hopes and spirits of all who would come to talk with her, and prepare them to help in the rescue and regeneration of the kingdom. This occupied every waking moment she had. But it was no matter. There was nothing she could not learn—and in the briefest time, too. Her horse would find this out in the first hour. Meantime the brothers and I took the horse in turn and began to learn to ride. And we had teaching in the use of the sword and other arms also. . . .

Joan's triumphant entrance into Orleans.

* * *

We were twenty-five strong, and well equipped. We rode in double file, Joan and her brothers in the center of the column, with Jean de Metz at the head of it and the Sieur Bertrand at its extreme rear. The knights were so placed to prevent desertions—for the present. In two or three hours we should be in the enemy's country, and then none would venture to desert. By and by we began to hear groans and sobs and execrations from different points along the line, and upon inquiry found that six of our men were peasants who had never ridden a horse before, and were finding it very difficult to stay in their saddles, and moreover were now beginning to suffer considerable bodily torture. They had been seized by the governor at the last moment and pressed into the service to make up the tale, and he had placed a veteran alongside of each with orders to help him stick to the saddle, and kill him if he tried to desert.

—*Personal Recollections of Joan of Arc* (1896), book 2, chapters 2–3

41

BRINGING UP THE REAR

This passage from The Innocents Abroad *is not really about any kind of war. It does, however, describe a moment during Mark Twain's expedition across the Holy Land when he and his traveling companions behaved as though they were riding in a military caravan that was about to be attacked. What Mark Twain says about his own behavior is similar to what he would later say about himself in "The Private History of a Campaign That Failed."*

The Jordan journey being approved, our dragoman [guide] was notified.

At nine in the morning the caravan was before the hotel door and we were at breakfast. There was a commotion about the place. Rumors of war and bloodshed were flying every where. The lawless Bedouins in the Valley of the Jordan and the deserts down by the Dead Sea were up in arms, and were going to destroy all comers. They had had a battle with a troop of Turkish cavalry and defeated them; several men killed. They had shut up the inhabitants of a village and a Turkish garrison in an old fort near Jericho, and were besieging them. They had marched upon a camp of our excursionists by the Jordan, and the pilgrims only saved their lives by stealing away and flying to Jerusalem under whip and spur in the darkness of the night. Another of our parties had been fired on from an ambush and then attacked in the open day. Shots were fired on both sides. Fortunately there was no bloodshed.

We spoke with the very pilgrim who had fired one of the shots, and learned from his own lips how, in this imminent deadly peril, only the cool courage of the pilgrims, their strength of numbers and imposing display of war material, had saved them from utter destruction. It was reported that the Consul had requested that no more of our pilgrims should go to the Jordan while this state of things lasted; and further, that he was unwilling that any more should go, at least without an unusually strong military guard. Here was trouble. But with the horses at the door and every body aware of what they were there for, what would you have done? Acknowledged that you were afraid, and backed shamefully out? Hardly. It would not be human nature, where there were so many women. You would have done as we did: said you were not afraid of a million Bedouins—and made your will and proposed quietly to yourself to take up an unostentatious position in the rear of the procession.

Everyone in the expedition gets down to check his saddle, as Mark Twain struggles to remain at the rear.

I think we must all have determined upon the same line of tactics, for it did seem as if we never would get to Jericho. I had a notoriously slow horse, but somehow I could not keep him in the rear, to save my neck. He was forever turning up in the lead. In such cases I trembled a little, and got down to fix my saddle. But it was not of any use. The others all got down to fix their saddles, too. I never saw such a time with saddles. It was the first time any of them had got out of order in three weeks, and now they had all broken down at once. I tried walking, for exercise—I had not had enough in Jerusalem searching for holy places. But it was a failure. The whole mob were suffering for exercise, and it was not fifteen minutes till they were all on foot and I had the lead again. It was very discouraging.

—*The Innocents Abroad* (1869), chapter 55

42

HORSES AND ARMOR MAKE A BAD MIX

Joan of Arc *may be the Mark Twain work saying the most about war, but the work saying the most about war horses is* A Connecticut Yankee in King Arthur's Court. *In that 1889 novel, Hank Morgan, a factory foreman, is mysteriously cast back into sixth-century England, where he introduces late-nineteenth-century American ideas and technology. This passage from the novel about the Yankee's preparations to ride off on a quest points out problems in combining horseback riding with wearing heavy armor—starting with simply mounting a horse. In fact, it wouldn't be an exaggeration to say that one of the reasons Mark Twain wrote this story was to have fun describing the petty annoyances of wearing armor, such as being unable to swat flies from one's nose, to perspire comfortably, or even to carry a basket of sandwiches on which to snack while on the road.*

I was to have an early breakfast, and start at dawn, for that was the usual way; but I had the demon's own time with my armor, and this delayed me a little. It is troublesome to get into, and there is so much detail. First you wrap a layer or two of blanket around your body, for a sort of cushion and to keep off the cold iron; then you put on your sleeves and shirt of chain mail—these are made of small steel links woven together, and they form a fabric so flexible that if you toss your shirt onto the floor, it slumps into a pile like a peck of wet fish-net; it is very heavy and is nearly the uncomfortablest material in the world for a night shirt, yet plenty used it for that—tax collectors, and reformers, and one-horse kings with a defective title, and those sorts of people; then you put on your shoes—flat-boats roofed over with interleaving bands of steel—and screw your clumsy spurs into the heels. Next you buckle your greaves on your legs, and your cuisses on your thighs; then come your backplate and your breastplate, and you begin to feel crowded; then you hitch onto the breastplate the half-petticoat of broad overlapping bands of steel which hangs down in front but is scolloped out behind so you can sit down, and isn't any real improvement on an inverted coal scuttle, either for looks or for wear, or to wipe your hands on; next you belt on your sword; then you put your stove-pipe joints onto your arms, your iron gauntlets onto your hands, your iron rat-trap onto your head, with a rag of steel web hitched onto it to hang over the back of your neck—and there you are, snug as a candle in a candle-mould. This is no time to dance. Well, a man that is packed away like that is a nut that isn't worth the cracking, there is so little of the meat, when you get down to it, by comparison with the shell.

Everyone waving goodbye.

The boys helped me, or I never could have got in. Just as we finished, Sir Bedivere happened in, and I saw that as like as not I hadn't chosen the most convenient outfit for a long trip. How stately he looked; and tall and broad and grand. He had on his head a conical steel casque that only came down to his ears, and for visor had only a narrow steel bar that extended down to his upper lip and protected his nose; and all the rest of him, from neck to heel, was flexible chain mail, trousers and all. But pretty much all of him was hidden under his outside garment, which of course was of chain mail, as I said, and hung straight from his shoulders to his ankles; and from his middle to the bottom, both before and behind, was divided, so that he could ride and let the skirts hang down on each side. He was going grailing, and it was just the outfit for it, too. I would have given a good deal for that ulster, but it was too late now to be fooling around. The sun was just up, the king and the court were all on hand to see me off and wish me luck; so it wouldn't be etiquette for me to tarry. You don't get on your horse yourself; no, if you tried it you would get disappointed. They carry you out, just as they carry a sun-struck man to the drug store, and put you on, and help get you to rights, and fix your feet in the stirrups; and all the while you do feel so strange and stuffy and like somebody else—like somebody that has been married on a sudden, or struck by lightning, or something like that, and hasn't quite fetched around yet, and is sort of numb, and can't just get his bearings. Then they stood up the mast they called a spear, in its socket by my left foot, and I gripped it with my hand; lastly they hung my shield around my neck, and I was all complete and ready to up anchor and get to sea. Everybody was as good to me as they could be, and a maid of honor gave me the stirrup-cup her own self. There was nothing more to do now, but for that damsel to get up behind me on a pillion, which she did, and put an arm or so around me to hold on.

And so we started, and everybody gave us a goodbye and waved their handkerchiefs or helmets. And everybody we met, going down the hill and through the village was respectful to us, except some shabby little boys on the outskirts. They said:

"Oh, what a guy!" And hove clods at us.

In my experience boys are the same in all ages. They don't respect anything, they don't care for anything or anybody. They say "Go up, baldhead" to the prophet going his unoffending way in the gray of antiquity; they sass me in the holy gloom of the Middle Ages; and I had seen them act the same way in [President James] Buchanan's administration; I remember, because I was there and helped. The prophet had his bears and settled with his boys; and I wanted to get down and settle with mine, but it wouldn't answer, because I couldn't have got up again. I hate a country without a derrick.

—*A Connecticut Yankee in King Arthur's Court* (1889), chapter 11

Will Rogers as the Yankee being lowered onto his horse in the 1931 film Connecticut Yankee.

43

"SLIM JIM" VS. THE TOWER OF IRON

The previous passage from A Connecticut Yankee *reveals some drawbacks to wearing heavy armor while going into battle on a horse. This passage reveals another major drawback—reduced agility. Several years after unintentionally insulting a short-tempered knight named Sagramor, Hank is forced to meet Sagramor in a potentially deadly joust. Their battle presents startling contrasts in their strategies, equipment, and—mostly notably—their mounts. Thanks in part to Hank's light and agile horse, the resulting confrontation proves to be a turning point in his campaign to modernize early medieval England.*

Down at our end there were but two tents; one for me, and another for my servants. At the appointed hour the king made a sign, and the heralds, in their tabards, appeared and made proclamation, naming the combatants and stating the cause of quarrel. There was a pause, then a ringing bugle-blast, which was the signal for us to come forth. All the multitude caught their breath, and an eager curiosity flashed into every face.

Out from his tent rode great Sir Sagramor, an imposing tower of iron, stately and rigid, his huge spear standing upright in its socket and grasped in his strong hand, his grand horse's face and breast cased in steel, his body clothed in rich trappings that almost dragged the ground—oh, a most noble picture. A great shout went up, of welcome and admiration.

And then out I came. But I didn't get any shout. There was a wondering and eloquent silence for a moment, then a great wave of laughter began to sweep along that human sea, but a warning bugle-blast cut its career short. I was in the simplest and comfortablest of gymnast costumes—flesh-colored tights from neck to heel, with blue silk puffings about my loins, and bareheaded. My horse was not above medium size, but he was alert, slender-limbed, muscled with watchsprings, and just a greyhound to go. He was a beauty, glossy as silk, and naked as he was when he was born, except for bridle and ranger-saddle.

The Yankee in his simple gymnast suit, mounted on his slender-limbed and well-muscled horse.

The iron tower and the gorgeous bed quilt came cumbrously but gracefully pirouetting down the lists, and we tripped lightly up to meet them. We halted; the tower saluted, I responded; then we wheeled and rode side by side to the grand-stand and faced our king and queen, to whom we made obeisance. The queen exclaimed:

"Alack, Sir Boss, wilt fight naked, and without lance or sword or—"

But the king checked her and made her understand, with a polite phrase or two, that this was none of her business. The bugles rang again; and we separated and rode to the ends of the lists, and took position. Now old Merlin stepped into view and cast a dainty web of gossamer threads over Sir Sagramor which turned him into Hamlet's ghost; the king made a sign, the bugles blew, Sir Sagramor laid his great lance in rest, and the next moment here he came thundering down the course with his veil flying out behind, and I went whistling through the air like an arrow to meet him—cocking my ear the while, as if noting the invisible knight's position and progress by hearing, not sight. A chorus of encouraging shouts burst out for him, and one brave voice flung out a heartening word for me—said:

"Go it, slim Jim!"

It was an even bet that Clarence [the Yankee's assistant] had procured that favor for me—and furnished the language, too. When that formidable lance-point was within a yard and a half of my breast I twitched my horse aside without an effort, and the big knight swept by, scoring a blank. I got plenty of applause that time. We turned, braced up, and down we came again. Another blank for the knight, a roar of applause for me. This same thing was repeated once more; and it fetched such a whirlwind of applause that Sir Sagramor lost his temper, and at once changed his tactics and set himself the task of chasing me down. Why, he hadn't any show in the world at that; it was a game of tag, with all the advantage on my side; I whirled out of his path with ease whenever I chose, and once I slapped him on the back as I went to the rear. Finally I took the chase into my own hands; and after that, turn, or twist, or do what he would, he was never able to get behind me again; he found himself always in front at the end of his maneuver. So he gave up that business and retired to his end of the lists. His temper was clear gone now, and he forgot himself and flung an insult at me which disposed of mine. I slipped my lasso from the horn of my saddle, and grasped the coil in my right hand. This time you should have seen him come!—it was a business trip, sure; by his gait there was blood in his eye. I was sitting

The Yankee's lassoing of Sir Sagramor caused a sensation!

my horse at ease, and swinging the great loop of my lasso in wide circles about my head; the moment he was under way, I started for him; when the space between us had narrowed to forty feet, I sent the snaky spirals of the rope a-cleaving through the air, then darted aside and faced about and brought my trained animal to a halt with all his feet braced under him for a surge. The next moment the rope sprang taut and yanked Sir Sagramor out of the saddle! Great Scott, but there was a sensation!

Unquestionably, the popular thing in this world is novelty. These people had never seen anything of that cowboy business before, and it carried them clear off their feet with delight. From all around and everywhere, the shout went up:

"Encore! encore!"

—*A Connecticut Yankee in King Arthur's Court* (1889), chapter 39

The joust's audience enjoys an epic encore when Hank uses his lasso to unsaddle seven more knights, including the renowned Sir Launcelot. His real opponent, however, is not so much the knights but Merlin the Magician, who steals his lasso, leaving him apparently defenseless. The vengeful and presumably still invisible Sir Sagramor then demands a rematch. This time, however, Hank stealthily shoots Sagramor with a pistol that no one sees or would even understand if they did see it. He then turns back a mass onslaught of five hundred knights by shooting enough of them to break their charge. He emerges as unquestioned victor over Merlin's magic and knight errantry—but his real trouble is yet to come.

44

STRAIGHT FROM THE HORSE'S MOUTH

In 1877, English author Anna Sewell published her only novel, Black Beauty, *an autobiographical story about a long-abused horse that became an all-time bestseller. The book's principal aim was to persuade people to treat horses more kindly. Nearly three decades later, Mark Twain was asked for a story that would help an anti-bullfighting campaign in Spain. That request prompted him to write "A Horse's Tale," which is broadly similar to* Black Beauty *in being about a long-suffering horse telling his own story.* Harper's Magazine *published it in 1906, and it was made into a book a year later. Mark Twain hoped the book would match* Black Beauty*'s success, but it is now nearly forgotten. A strange story that is actually—and at times confusingly—narrated by multiple characters, it opens at a western US Cavalry post, with the title character himself—Soldier Boy—telling his own story.*

SOLDIER BOY–PRIVATELY TO HIMSELF

I am Buffalo Bill's horse. I have spent my life under his saddle—with him in it, too, and he is good for two hundred pounds, without his clothes; and there is no telling how much he does weigh when he is out on the war-path and has his batteries belted on. He is over six feet, is young, hasn't an ounce of waste flesh, is straight, graceful, springy in his motions, quick as a cat, and has a handsome face, and black hair dangling down on his shoulders, and is beautiful to look at; and nobody is braver than he is, and nobody is stronger, except myself. Yes, a person that doubts that he is fine to see should see him in his beaded buckskins, on my back and his rifle peeping above his shoulder, chasing a hostile trail, with me going like the wind and his hair streaming out behind from the shelter of his broad slouch. Yes, he is a sight to look at then—and I'm part of it myself.

I am his favorite horse, out of dozens. Big as he is, I have carried him eighty-one miles between nightfall and sunrise on the scout; and I am good for fifty, day in and day out, and all the time. I am not large, but I am built on a business basis. I have carried him thousands and thousands of miles on scout duty for the army, and there's not a gorge, nor a pass, nor a valley, nor a fort, nor a trading post, nor a buffalo-range in the whole sweep of the Rocky Mountains and the Great Plains that we don't know as well as we know the bugle-calls. He is Chief of Scouts to the Army of the Frontier, and it makes us very important. In such a position as I hold in the military service one needs to be of good family and possess an education much above the common to be worthy of the place. I am the best educated horse outside of the hippodrome, everybody says, and the best-mannered. It may be so, it is not for me to say; modesty is the best policy, I think. Buffalo Bill taught me the most of what I know, my mother taught me much, and I taught myself the rest. Lay a row of moccasins before me—Pawnee, Sioux, Shoshone, Cheyenne, Blackfoot, and as many other tribes as you please—and I can name the tribe every moccasin belongs to by the make of it. Name it in horse-talk, and could do it in American if I had speech.

Soldier Boy could name the Indian tribe of every moccasin he saw.

I know some of the Indian signs—the signs they make with their hands, and by signal-fires at night and columns of smoke by day. Buffalo Bill taught me how to drag wounded soldiers out of the line of fire with my teeth; and I've done it, too; at least I've dragged *him* out of the battle when he was wounded. And not just once, but twice. Yes, I know a lot of things. I remember forms, and gaits, and faces; and you can't disguise a person that's done me a kindness so that I won't know him thereafter wherever I find him. I know the art of searching for a trail, and I know the stale track from the fresh. I can keep a trail all by myself, with Buffalo Bill asleep in the saddle; ask him—he will tell you so. Many a time, when he has ridden all night, he has said to me at dawn, "Take the watch, Boy; if the trail freshens, call me." Then he goes to sleep. He knows he can trust me, because I have a reputation. A scout horse that has a reputation does not play with it.

My mother was all American—no alkali-spider about *her*, I can tell you; she was of the best blood of Kentucky, the bluest Blue-grass aristocracy, very proud and acrimonious—or maybe it is ceremonious. I don't know which it is. But it is no matter; size is the main thing about a word, and that one's up to standard. She spent her military life as colonel of the Tenth Dragoons, and saw a deal of rough service—distinguished service it was, too. I mean, she *carried* the Colonel; but it's all the same. Where would he be without his horse? He wouldn't arrive. It takes two to make a colonel of dragoons. She was a fine dragoon horse, but never got above that. She was strong enough for the scout service, and had the endurance, too, but she couldn't quite come up to the speed required; a scout horse has to have steel in his muscle and lightning in his blood.

My father was a bronco. Nothing as to lineage—that is, nothing as to recent lineage—but plenty good enough when you go a good way back. When Professor Marsh was out here hunting bones for the chapel of Yale University he found skeletons of horses no bigger than a fox, bedded in the rocks, and he said they were ancestors of my father. My mother heard him say it; and he said those skeletons were two million years old, which astonished her and made her Kentucky pretensions look small and pretty antiphonal, not to say oblique. Let me see . . . I used to know the meaning of those words, but . . . well, it was years ago, and 'tisn't as vivid now as it was when they were fresh. That sort of words doesn't keep, in the kind of climate we have out here. Professor Marsh said those skeletons were fossils. So that makes me part blue grass and part fossil; if there is any older or better stock, you will have to look for it among the Four Hundred, I reckon. I am satisfied with it. And am a happy horse, too, though born out of wedlock.

And now we are back at Fort Paxton once more, after a forty-day scout, away up as far as the Big Horn. Everything quiet. Crows and

Blackfeet squabbling—as usual—but no outbreaks, and settlers feeling fairly easy. The Seventh Cavalry still in garrison, here; also the Ninth Dragoons, two artillery companies, and some infantry. All glad to see me, including General Alison, commandant. The officers' ladies and children well, and called upon me—with sugar. Colonel Drake, Seventh Cavalry, said some pleasant things; Mrs. Drake was very complimentary; also Captain and Mrs. Marsh, Company B, Seventh Cavalry; also the Chaplain, who is always kind and pleasant to me, because I kicked the lungs out of a trader once. It was Tommy Drake and Fanny Marsh that furnished the sugar-nice children, the nicest at the post, I think.

That poor orphan child [Cathy Alison] is on her way from France—everybody is full of the subject. Her father was General Alison's brother; married a beautiful young Spanish lady ten years ago, and has never been in America since. They lived in Spain a year or two, then went to France. Both died some months ago. This little girl that is coming is the only child. General Alison is glad to have her. He has never seen her. He is a very nice old bachelor, but is an old bachelor just the same and isn't more than about a year this side of retirement by age limit; and so what does he know about taking care of a little maid nine years old? If I could have her it would be another matter, for I know all about children, and they adore me. Buffalo Bill will tell you so himself.

I have some of this news from overhearing the garrison-gossip, the rest of it I got from Potter, the General's dog. Potter is the great Dane. He is privileged, all over the post, like Shekels, the Seventh Cavalry's dog, and visits everybody's quarters and picks up everything that is going, in the way of news. Potter has no imagination, and no great deal of culture, perhaps, but he has a historical mind and a good memory, and so he is the person I depend upon mainly to post me up when I get back from a scout. That is, if Shekels is out on depredation and I can't get hold of him.

The orphan girl Cathy astride Soldier Boy, next to Buffalo Bill.

—*A Horse's Tale* (1906), chapter 1

45

A ROUGH RIDER ON WHEELS

Mark Twain eventually became a fervent anti-imperialist and harsh critic of Theodore Roosevelt's presidency, which began less than a year after he spoke the following words in late 1900. Only a week earlier, New York's then-governor Roosevelt had been elected vice president of the United States. At that time, Mark Twain still admired the man and couldn't resist commenting on the rapid political rise of several "Rough Riders," whom Roosevelt had led to glory in Cuba two years earlier. This passage answers the question about what kind of steed Mark Twain would want to ride if he were to become a Rough Rider.

Mark Twain going to war on an automobile.

Why, I could have been a Rough Rider myself if I had known that this political Klondike was going to open up, and I would have been a Rough Rider if I could have gone to war on an automobile—but not on a horse! No, I know the horse too well; I have known the horse in war and in peace, and there is no place where a horse is comfortable. The horse has too many caprices, and he is too much given to initiative. He invents too many new ideas. No, I don't want anything to do with a horse.

—address to the Lotos Club, November 10, 1900

"A donkey *had gotten the best of our father!"*

PART IX

CLOSER TO HOME AND FAMILY

Most of the chapters in this book are about horse-related episodes that Mark Twain experienced during his travels to faraway places. The chapters in this section differ because they concern incidents closer to home, and a few involve family members in other places. Several passages come from his daughter Clara's biography of him—the most intimate account of Mark Twain's life by anyone other than himself. Horses and their kin dominated land transportation around the world throughout Mark Twain's life, so it is not surprising that he and his family were rarely far from them, even in their Hartford home—where some of these incidents took place.

THE PROFANE OSTLER

In 1874, while on a walking tour with his friend the Reverend Joseph Twichell, Mark Twain and his companion stopped at a tavern whose rustic patrons glared at them with disinterested silence. Eager to strike up a conversation, the reverend guessed from the room's decor and smells that one of the other men "might possibly be coaxed into a state of semi-interest by some reference to horses. . . . So he said, 'Well, ostler, I suppose you raise some pretty fine breeds of horses around here?'

"The young fellow unbent right away; and his face, which was a good face, lighted pleasantly, eagerly in fact. He untitled, planted his feet on the floor, shoved his coon tail around to the rear, spread his broad hands upon his knees, beamed up at the tall Reverend, and turned himself loose:

"'Well, now, I tell you!—pretty fine ain't the word!—and it don't begin!'

"Evidently he was as good-hearted a young fellow as ever was, and as guiltless of wish or intent to offend; yet into the chance chinks of that single little short sentence he managed to wattle as much as two yards and a half of the most varied and wonderful profanity! And that sentence did not end his speech—no, it was the mere introduction; straight after it followed the speech—a speech five minutes long, full of enthusiastic horse statistics; poured out with the most fluent facility, as from an inexhaustible crater, and all ablaze from beginning to end with crimson lava jets of desolating and utterly unconscious profanity! It was his native tongue; he had no idea that there was any harm in it."

—*Mark Twain in Eruption*, "Miscellany"

46

MILK RUN

The horseback ride on the island of Hawaii that Mark Twain describes here really happened in 1866. What he adds about an earlier event in his life, however, must fall under the heading of apocryphal. Not only is there no corroborating evidence for its authenticity, but it's also difficult to think of any moment in Mark Twain's life when it could have occurred! Nevertheless, it is an engaging story.

We rode horseback all around the island of Hawaii (the crooked road making the distance two hundred miles), and enjoyed the journey very much. We were more than a week making the trip, because our Kanaka horses would not go by a house or a hut without stopping—whip and spur could not alter their minds about it, and so we finally found that it economized time to let them have their way. Upon inquiry the mystery was explained: the natives are such thorough-going gossips that they never pass a house without stopping to swap news, and consequently their horses learn to regard that sort of thing as an essential part of the whole duty of man, and his salvation not to be compassed without it. However, at a former crisis of my life I had once taken an aristocratic young lady out driving, behind a horse that had just retired from a long and honorable career as the moving impulse of a milk wagon, and so this present experience awoke a reminiscent sadness in me in place of the exasperation more

natural to the occasion. I remembered how helpless I was that day, and how humiliated; how ashamed I was of having intimated to the girl that I had always owned the horse and was accustomed to grandeur; how hard I tried to appear easy, and even vivacious, under suffering that was consuming my vitals; how placidly and maliciously the girl smiled, and kept on smiling, while my hot blushes baked themselves into a permanent blood-pudding in my face; how the horse ambled from one side of the street to the other and waited complacently before every third house two minutes and a quarter while I belabored his back and reviled him in my heart; how I tried to keep him from turning corners, and failed; how I moved heaven and earth to get him out of town, and did not succeed; how he traversed the entire settlement and delivered imaginary milk at a hundred and sixty-two different domiciles, and how he finally brought up at a dairy depot and refused to budge further, thus rounding and completing the revealment of what the plebeian service of his life had been; how, in eloquent silence, I walked the girl home, and how, when I took leave of her, her parting remark scorched my soul and appeared to blister me all over: she said that my horse was a fine, capable animal, and I must have taken great comfort in him in my time—but that if I would take along some milk-tickets next time, and appear to deliver them at the various halting places, it might expedite his movements a little. There was a coolness between us after that.

—*Roughing It* (1872), chapter 76

47

CLARA'S MAGIC CALF

The Hartford home in which Mark Twain raised his daughters generally had more than its share of cats, dogs, carriage horses, and other critters. In her biography of her father, Clara Clemens recalls a calf the family once owned. It made a lovely pet, but what Clara really wanted was a horse of her own.

Another pronounced character in the household was the coachman [Patrick McAleer]. He persuaded me that if I curried the calf every morning and put a saddle and bridle on him he would turn into a horse. The idea seemed marvelous to me and I was always ready to believe in miracles, even at the age of six.

I can't remember whether either of my parents knew of this transformation which was to take place in the calf, but I do recall that I had to keep one dress especially for the stable, because the perfumes I brought into the house with me did not seem to attract anyone. I loved the smell of the barn, but the other members of my family plainly showed they did not.

Smelling the hay and horses was, in fact, the pleasantest part of my labor, for I suffered great fatigue from trying to reach up high enough to brush and comb the top parts of the calf. One of the servants, becoming interested in my efforts, gave me an old piece of billiard-cloth of Father's. Perfectly delighted, I draped "Jumbo" (my calf) in this brilliant green covering. After that, the coachman, the calf, and I went for a walk on the avenue, to the amazement of passers-by. These promenades never lasted long, however, for "Jumbo" was much too lively for my safety. Of course, "Jumbo's" horns kept growing, which seemed to me very strange, but the coachman assured me that later they would drop out. Eventually, a saddle and bridle were bought and I mounted my restless steed. Needless to say, I was hurled into the nearest bush, before I could even give thanks for my new pony.

Two ejections from that obstinate back discouraged me and I retreated to my nursery. I loved the animal still, however. Therefore,

It seemed very strange to Clara that Jumbo's horns kept growing.

when Patrick, the coachman, confessed to me, when I appeared in the barn as usual the morning following my second "throw," that he had sold "Jumbo," I raised such a hullaballoo that my screams reached even my father's study. He came running down to snatch me from danger. When he discovered the cause of my misery, he was most sympathetic and told Patrick he would have to buy the calf back immediately; which was done that very day. Father could always be depended upon to see that the fair thing was done, and although he had no particular liking for cows, big or little, he loved animals in general and could understand the pain I felt in being separated from my pet.

—Clara Clemens, *My Father, Mark Twain* (1931), chapter 3

THE GIFT HORSE

A recollection of Mark Twain's forty-third birthday in 1878, when his daughter Clara was four and a half and Susy was six and a half.

This morning when Clara discovered that this is my birthday, she was greatly troubled because she had provided no gift for me, and repeated her sorrow several times. Finally she went musing to the nursery and presently returned with her newest and dearest treasure, a large toy horse, and said, "You shall have this horse for your birthday, papa."

I accepted it with many thanks. After an hour she was racing up and down the room with the horse, when Susy said, "Why Clara, you gave that horse to papa, and now you've tooken it again."

Clara.—"I never give it to him for always; I give it to him for his birthday."

—"Chapters from My Autobiography" (1907), chapter 19

MY FATHER MARK TWAIN

by CLARA CLEMENS

WITH HITHERTO UNPUBLISHED LETTERS OF MARK TWAIN

ILLUSTRATED FROM FAMILY PHOTOGRAPHS

HARPER & BROTHERS ESTABLISHED 1817

48

HOW NOT TO RIDE A DONKEY

Clara's biography of her father also contains this vivid reminiscence of other family pets, which included a cantankerous donkey named Kadichan (a.k.a. Kiditchin). Perhaps recalling his pleasant rides on donkeys during the Quaker City *excursion years earlier, Mark Twain couldn't resist demonstrating to his daughters the proper way to ride a donkey. They weren't impressed.*

Except for the birthday party at my grandmother's, very little social life was courted by any of the family. My sisters and I were not allowed to go to parties and our parents sought solitude and repose during the summer months on the lovely farm. There was plenty of companionship with animals, however. Of these there were represented various species in the household, both wild and tame. Starting with dogs large enough to be harnessed and pull a little express-cart, we progressed to a couple of donkeys (called "Kadichan" and "Polichon") and, finally, graduated in patience and courage with a pair of ponies in our possession.

Although Father's pet animals were the cats and kittens, to which he gave much attention, he was also interested in our various experiences with the more important four-footed animals, and offered to lend a hand when the donkeys were obstreperous. In one particular case the larger donkey, "Kadichan" (named after the delightful book, *Adventures with*

Perhaps not a fan of Mark Twain's poetry, Kadichan neatly deposited the poet on the ground.

a Donkey), made a ten-strike.* The only way my sisters and I had ever succeeded in forcing the animal to go was for one to sit on him while the other walked ahead with a bag of crackers just out of reach of his nose. Of course this meant a lot of discussion as to whose "turn" it was to walk with the crackers, particularly on a very hot day.

Once Father had been listening to our arguments from the porch, when he suddenly joined us with one-hundred-per-cent determination in his eye.

"I'll make that creature do his work," he said, in a tone that sounded almost like a boast, and up he jerked himself into the saddle. But "Kadichan" moved one great ear forward in visible protest and, dropping

* Sophie, Countess of Ségur, *The Adventures of a Donkey* (1860; English trans. 1880).

his head as he raised his hind legs ever so little, he deposited my father in the long grass in front of him. The whole transaction lasted only a second, but Father's bewildered expression of face, as he lay on his back in the grass, engraved an indelible picture in our minds. A donkey had gotten the best of our father! We giggled ourselves to sleep that night and Father was in good spirits, too. He said he was "more attracted to the donkey than ever before, because the power to accompany an act of vengeance with so much grace and serenity proved the animal to be superhuman."

—Clara Clemens, *My Father, Mark Twain* (1931), chapter 5

When Mark Twain's oldest daughter, Susy, was thirteen, she started to write a book about her father containing this poem that he wrote about the pet donkey Kadichan.

KIDITCHIN

O du lieb' Kiditchin
Du bist ganz bewitchin,
Waw— he!

In summer days Kiditchin
Thou'rt dear from nose to britchin
Waw—he!

No dought thoult get a switchin
When for mischief thou'rt itchin'
Waw—he!

But when you're good Kiditchin
You shall feast in James's kitchin
Waw—he!

O now lift up thy song—
Thy noble note prolong—
Thou living Chinese gong!
  Waw—he! waw—he waw
  Sweetest donkey man ever saw.

—Albert Bigelow Paine,
Mark Twain: A Biography (1912), chapter 157

In a postscript to the poem, Paine added that when the donkey threw him over her head, Mark Twain "thought she might have been listening to the poem he had written of her."

49

PREVENTING CRUELTY TO ANIMALS

In this extract from her biography of her father, Clara recalls an experience she and her sister Jean had trying to protect an abused draft horse when the family was in Paris in 1893. Mark Twain was normally a strong advocate of treating animals kindly, but his daughters' time-consuming Good Samaritan efforts demonstrated there were limits to his patience.

My younger sister, Jean, and I had hastened to become members of the Society for Prevention of Cruelty to Animals a few days after arriving in Paris. We were very proud of the blue cards enabling us to cut short the beating of any horse on the street, whether driven by a private coachman or a coal-wagon driver. We were kept extremely busy at our task, too, for in both France and Italy little love is wasted on the dumb beasts. But father, although theoretically in sympathy with our new profession, found it extremely inconvenient at times. For instance, it happened once or twice that when Jean and I were driving with him to some important social function, the driver started to beat the horse. Naturally out flew our blue cards, which we were never without, and after much agitated conversation with the coachman he was made to understand he could choose between one more blow on the horse's back or prison. While the conversation had progressed the horse stood still, and now without the whip it was hard to start him again. We made little headway. The horse walked us the rest of the way, so that we gave the appearance of driving at a funeral. Finally Father lost his temper completely and jumped out of the carriage, calling back to us: "Girls, you can drive the other two blocks alone; I wouldn't go to hell at such a pace."

—Clara Clemens, *My Father, Mark Twain* (1931), chapter 8

Mark Twain's most intimate friend, Joseph Twichell, once said of him, "I never knew a person so finely regardful of the feelings of others in some ways. . . . [His] sensitive regard for others extends to animals. When we are driving his concern is all about the horse. He can't bear to see the whip used, or to see a horse pull hard" (Albert Bigelow Paine, *Mark Twain: A Biography* [1912], chapter 118).

50

THE MOST PRECIOUS HORSES IN THE WORLD

Mark Twain's beloved wife, Livy, died on June 5, 1904, while his family was residing in Florence, Italy. Exactly one week later, he wrote to his brother-in-law Charles J. Langdon, explaining that he was having two horses that Livy had bought for Clara and Jean shipped home to the United States. A week later, he followed with the following letter, paying a moving tribute to those horses.

Dear Charley:

I am a man without a country. Wherever Livy was, that was my country. And now she is gone. It is 2 weeks to-day. But it seems only yesterday. Tomorrow we quit this residence-without her. Tomorrow we quit this residence—without her. That is strange: it has never happened before. For four days the trunk-packing has been going on—and Livy not superintending. *That* has never happened before: for even when we were leaving Riverdale she gave instructions from her bed. We have had to do all our planning by ourselves; for our journey, & if she were here she would show us that we have done it poorly, & we should see it ourselves. We have been beset with perplexities and uncertainties—she never had any. How we miss her clear head! . . .

I am bringing nothing dutiable except a couple of side-saddles, which the children have used several months. If they are dutiable, all right; I think they cost Livy $30 or $40 apiece. They & the horses were her last important gift to the children. She wouldn't let me share—she paid the whole out of her own Elmira money, & took such an enthusiastic pleasure in it. Those are the most precious horses in the world, now.

—letter to Charles J. Langdon, June 19, 1904

Clara Clemens riding sidesaddle on the horse her mother gave her in Italy.

51

THE MAUDE SQUAD

Mark Twain's last equine encounters occurred on the island of Bermuda, which he loved to visit. He opens the reminiscence here with comments about a young American girl named Margaret Blackmer, with whom he spent considerable time during his 1908 sojourn on the island. Their main form of transportation was a small cart pulled by a dignified little donkey named Maude. (This is not quite a family story—unless, that is, one considers Margaret and other young girls whom Mark Twain made his "Angelfish" to have been his surrogate granddaughters.)

We were close comrades—inseparables in fact—for eight days. Every day we made pedestrian excursions—called them that anyway, and honestly they were intended for that, and that is what they would have been but for the persistent intrusion of a gray and grave and rough-coated little donkey by the name of Maude. Maude was four feet long; she was mounted on four slender little stilts, and had ears that doubled her altitude when she stood them up straight. Which she seldom did. Her ears were a most interesting study. She was always expressing her private thoughts and opinions with them, and doing it with such nice shadings, and so intelligibly, that she had no need of speech whereby to reveal her mind. This was all new to me. The donkey had always been a sealed book to me before, but now I saw that I could read this one as easily as I could read coarse print. Sometimes she would throw those ears straight forward, like the prongs of a fork; under the impulse of a fresh emotion she would lower the starboard one to a level; next she would stretch it backward till it pointed nor'-nor'east; next she would retire it to due east, and presently clear down to south-east-by-south—all these changes revealing her thoughts to me without her suspecting it. She always worked the port ear for a quite different set of emotions, and sometimes she would fetch both ears rearward till they were level and became a fork, the one prong pointing southeast the other southwest.

She was a most interesting little creature, and always self-possessed, always dignified, always resisting authority; never in agreement with anybody, and if she ever smiled once during the eight days I did not catch her at it. Her tender was a little bit of a cart with seat room for two in it, and you could fall out of it without knowing it, it was so close to the ground. This battery was in command of a nice grave, dignified, gentle-faced little black boy whose age was about twelve, and whose name, for some reason or other, was Reginald.

—*Autobiography of Mark Twain*, vol. 3 (2015)

Mark Twain and one of his "Angelfish" girls riding in a cart pulled by Maude, under young Reginald's direction.

Elizabeth Wallace, another American whom Mark Twain befriended in Bermuda, wrote a book about him and the island, including additional anecdotes about Maude.

That afternoon Margaret went with Mr. Clemens in the donkey-cart. I saw them start, or, rather, try to start. For Maude was stubborn and it took some time to persuade her to move. Maude was diminutive in size, but the amount of obstinacy she possessed would have fitted out a mastodon, nicely. She was always attached to a small cart, and early every morning she was at her post in front of the hotel. She showed perfect indifference as to whether she went or came. Of course, she preferred a stationary attitude. Reginald was her guardian angel—a black little islander who enjoyed the distinction of being the only human being who could make Maude go. . . .

One morning, when we were returning after a happy jaunt, Mr. [Henry H.] Rogers began to berate Mr. Clemens for riding longer than was his turn. Mr. Clemens defended himself by saying that it was purely out of consideration for Maude, as his light weight could not discourage her, whereas Mr. Rogers's heavy form would be a burden too great for her. The result of the discussion was that Mr. Rogers and I got into the cart, while Mr. Clemens, the Angelfish, and the others walked behind. Despite our efforts, Maude could not be made to see the advantage of going rapidly, and when we came to the hill in front of the hotel she stopped completely and went down on her knees—her final argument. I tender-heartedly suggested getting out and helping Maude up the incline. But Mr. Rogers had a happier plan, which was to make Mr. Clemens push the cart up the hill. Mr. Clemens demurred at first, but submitted with good grace, and Maude, encouraged by the sympathetic friend in the rear, pricked up her long, sad ears, and we dashed up to the front entrance in fine style, with the Angelfish following fast behind.

—Elizabeth Wallace, *Mark Twain and the Happy Island* (1913), chapters 2 and 8

Mark, Margaret, and Maude.

IMAGE CREDITS

Beard, Daniel, *Connecticut Yankee in King Arthur's Court* (Charles Webster & Co., 1889), pp. 164, 168, 169.

Beard, Daniel, *Following the Equator* (Harper & Bros., 1897), p. 24.

Connecticut Yankee, A (Fox Film Corp., 1931), p. 166.

Fraser, F. A., *Roughing It* (Chatto & Windus, 1872), pp. 10, 11, 116

Hitchcock, Lucius Wolcott, *A Horse's Tale* (Harper & Bros., 1907), pp. x, xiv, 174.

Kemble, E. W., *Adventures of Huckleberry Finn* (Charles Webster & Co., 1885), p. 135.

Mac Donnell, Kevin, private collection, p. 192.

Scherrer, Jean-Jacques, *Personal Recollections of Joan of Arc* (Harper & Bros., 1896), p. 160.

Unknown, *Life on the Mississippi* (James R. Osgood & Co., 1883), pp. 88, 111.

Wallace, Elizabeth, *Mark Twain and the Happy Island* (A. C. McClurg & Co., 1913), pp. 194, 196.

Williams, True, *The Innocents Abroad* (American Publ. Co., 1869), pp. 40, 58, 60, 74, 84, 104, 162.

Williams, True, *Roughing It* (American Publ. Co., 1872), frontispiece, pp. 70, 122, 141, 142, 180.

Williams, True, *A Tramp Abroad* (American. Publ. Co., 1880), pp. 64–65.

All other illustrations are AI images created by the editor using Microsoft Bing's online Image Creator program.

ACKNOWLEDGMENTS

Nearly ten years ago, when I composed the acknowledgments for *Mark Twain for Dog Lovers*, I mentioned having prepared a proposal for a book to be called *Mark Twain for Horse Lovers* that I called an "equine gem." I also remarked that the proposal was "on hold for the moment," never imagining that "moment" would last as long as it has. I now believe I was correct in calling that long, dormant proposal a gem, for I honestly feel that the present volume may be the most entertaining collection of Mark Twain's writings about animals yet published. The reason for that, of course, is that Mark Twain wrote so many witty and compelling things about horses and their kin. And for doing that, I must sincerely thank him.

In the introduction to this book, I raise the question of whether Mark Twain himself truly loved horses as much as he loved animals such as cats and dogs, and I suggest that the answer might be no. Those who have read this entire book up to this point may have their own answers to that question, so instead of pushing my own views on the subject, I'll instead pose a different question: If Mark Twain truly did love horses, would what he had to say about them be as interesting as what he actually said? My answer to that question is no. One of my favorite quotes from this collection is *"I never mount a horse without experiencing a sort of dread that I may be setting out on that last mysterious journey which all of us must take sooner or later."* Personally, I find a comment like that far more engaging than something like this: *"I love horses so much that I experience unbounded joy every time I mount one."* I would admire anyone who actually thinks that way about horses, but for unbounded pleasure in reading, give me Mark Twain every time.

Next, I must thank my wonderful agent, Charlotte Gusay, for sticking by me this past decade and for her unrelenting encouragement in every project I have undertaken. I would also like to thank the editorial director of Lyons Press, Rick Rinehart, for unhesitatingly endorsing this book the moment I dusted off and presented my old proposal to him. Nicole Myers deserves my thanks for patiently serving as the book's production editor and putting up with me through a process that has proved more difficult than either of us expected. I would also like to thank two of my most supportive Mark Twain allies, Barbara Schmidt and Kevin Mac Donnell, with whom I've had the pleasure of collaborating on several other books. As always, they have helped make this book better with their help and advice.

Finally, I must say a few words about the book's illustrations, many of which are photo-realistic AI (artificial intelligence) images. I created all but one of these images myself using Microsoft's seemingly miraculous online program Bing Image Creator, for which I thank Microsoft heartily. The illustrations in my previous Lyons Press book, *Mark Twain's Tales of the Macabre & Mysterious*, are products of Bing. Many readers loved them, while others would have preferred that I used nothing but line drawings produced for Mark Twain's original books. I have sought a middle ground for the present volume by selecting more than thirty of the best available original illustrations, including several real photographs (one of which is published here for the first time), and supplementing them with Bing AI illustrations. It is my hope that readers will appreciate the fact that about forty of the AI pictures illustrate texts for which no original illustrations exist.

ABOUT THE EDITOR

R. Kent Rasmussen is a retired reference-book editor who lives in Thousand Oaks, California. A graduate of the University of California at Berkeley, where the Mark Twain Papers are housed, he also earned a doctorate in history at UCLA, where he later taught and worked as associate editor of the Marcus Garvey Papers. In addition to editing scores of reference books on a wide variety of subjects, he has written extensively on history and on Mark Twain. *Mark Twain for Horse Lovers* is his third book for Lyons Press. It is also his fourteenth book on Mark Twain overall, and he is currently working on his fifteenth, again for Lyons Press. The recipient of numerous awards for his reference books, he was recognized in 2015 as a Legacy Scholar in the *Mark Twain Journal*, of which he is a board member, and he received the Mark Twain Circle of America's Thomas A. Tenney Award for Service in 2019.

Rasmussen is well known for his books on African history, but he is even better known as the author of the award-winning *Mark Twain A to Z* (1995, revised as the two-volume *Critical Companion to Mark Twain* in 2007). It and Rasmussen's other books have been praised for their compelling and often lively writing, which are on display in the present volume. His other Mark Twain books include *Mark Twain's Book for Bad Boys and Girls* (1995), *The Quotable Mark Twain* (1997), *Mark Twain for Kids* (2004), *Bloom's How to Write about Mark Twain* (2008), *Critical Insights: Mark Twain* (2011), *Dear Mark Twain: Letters from His Readers*

(2013), *Mark Twain and Youth* (2016, coedited with Kevin Mac Donnell), *Critical Insights: Adventures of Huckleberry Finn* (2017), *Critical Insights: The Adventures of Tom Sawyer* (2022), and *Mark Twain's Tales of the Macabre & Mysterious* (2024). Others of his books include *World War I for Kids* (2014) and *World War II: Q&A* (2021).

Rasmussen's other publications include introductions and notes for the Penguin Classics editions of *Tom Sawyer* (2014), *Huckleberry Finn* (2014), and Mark Twain's *Autobiographical Writings* (2012). Over the past seven years, he has also written extensively about screen adaptations of Mark Twain's writings in articles for other books and journals. He hopes eventually to publish a comprehensive book on that subject.

www.ingramcontent.com/pod-product-compliance
Lightning Source LLC
Chambersburg PA
CBHW020321030826
48979CB00022B/631

* 9 7 8 1 4 9 3 0 9 1 7 2 0 *